ROMMEL
THE
DESERT
WARRIOR

FRANCE

SPAIN

Po

Genoa

CORSICA

APENNINES

Tiber

Rome

SARDINIA

ITALY

ADRIATIC SEA

YUGOSLAVIA

ALBANIA

Taranto

MEDITERRANEAN

SICILY

Bizerta

Tunis

Algiers

Enfidaville

MALTA

Sfax

ALGERIA

Marelli

Medenine

Zuara

Tripoli

TUNISIA

Zaula

Homs

GULF OF SIDRA

Tarhuna

Buerat

Sirte

TRIPOLITANIA

LIBYA

Nofilia

El Aghella

WESTERN

THE BATTLEGROUND OF
ROMMEL'S AFRIKA KORPS

0   100   200 Miles

100   200 Kilometers

ROMMEL
THE
DESERT
WARRIOR

The Afrika Korps in World War II

Richard L. Blanco

Julian Messner
New York

15623

Manufactured in the United States of America.

Design by Irving Perkins Associates

Photos, Courtesy Imperial War Museum, London

Library of Congress Cataloging in Publication Data
Blanco, Richard L.
  Rommel, the desert warrior.
  Bibliography: p.
  Includes index.
  *Summary: Traces the World War II career of the
"Desert Fox," commander of the German Afrika
Corps, finally defeated by the British at el-
Alamein.*
  *1. World War, 1939–1945—Campaigns—Africa,
North—Juvenile literature. 2. Rommel, Erwin,
1891–1944—Juvenile literature. 3. World War,
1939–1945—Regimental histories—Germany—
Panzerarmeekorps Afrika—Juvenile literature.
4. Germany. Heer. Panzerarmeekorps Afrika—
History—Juvenile literature. [1. World War,
1939–1945—Campaigns—Africa, North. 2. Rommel,
Erwin, 1891–1944. 3. Germany—History, Military]
I. Title.*
D766.82.B573   940.54'23   82–2293
ISBN 0–671–42245–6   AACR2

ACKNOWLEDGMENTS

I AM particularly grateful to Jane L. Reid for drawing the maps for this book. To Brenda Peake and Christine Change I am obligated for typing my drafts. To J. S. Lucas, Deputy Head of the Department of Photographs, Imperial War Museum, London, I am indebted for the photographs in this book. I thank the Keeper of the Department of Photographs, Imperial War Museum, London, for permission to reproduce photographs from the museum's collection.

I dedicate this book to my son Rick who taught me, in my mellowing years, to run, to ski, and to backpack. I shall always be particularly grateful to him for our last wilderness adventure together—that wonderful canoe trip in Canada.

CONTENTS

1
THE SETTING

DURING WORLD War II the armies of Germany, Italy, and Japan fought numerous campaigns against the forces of the Allied nations. One contest in the struggle was unique. No combat was more unusual than the desert war fought in Libya and Egypt by the Germans and the Italians against the armies of the British Commonwealth between 1940 and 1943. Here, in a vast desolate terrain, the Afrika Korps, led by Field Marshal Erwin Rommel, conducted a new form of warfare characterized by speed, mobility, and deception. Combat here matched the Afrika Korps, consisting of German and Italian troops, against the British Eighth Army, which was composed of Englishmen, Irishmen, Welshmen, Scotsmen, Australians, New Zealanders, South Africans, Indians, and the Free French, as well as Jews, Poles, and Greeks.

In June 1940 the conquest of France completed Germany's domination of western Europe, and Great Britain barely managed to salvage its expeditionary force from Dunkirk on the French coast. Now the British nation prepared for an invasion by Adolf Hitler's divisions massing on the shores of the English Channel. Fighting in the air against attacks by the Luftwaffe (the German air force) and at sea against packs of enemy U-boats (submarines) that hunted Allied cargoes, Britain was struggling for its life. The nation was entirely dependent on oil imported from the Middle East, and Egypt

—the shield for Britain's petroleum refineries—was vital for survival.

After the cross-channel assault on England by German troops was postponed that autumn as a result of the heroic defense put up by the British Royal Air Force, the action switched to the Western Desert of North Africa. Here a torrid wasteland stretches 150 miles from the Mediterranean southward to the Sahara, embracing two-thirds of Egypt and half of Libya. In this new arena, desert combat was waged on a massive scale for the first time in the twentieth century. Here the tide of battle—sometimes favoring the Axis (the Germans and Italians), sometimes the Allies—ebbed and flowed for three years in one of the most dramatic episodes in modern military history.

Desert fighting provided a new dimension to warfare. It offered ample opportunities for wide flanking, daring maneuvers, and tactical procedures with mechanized equipment unmatched in Europe. The northern edge of this great area was bounded by the sparkling waters of the Mediterranean, but the southern end was wide open, extending many miles into bleak terrain. The Western Desert is a lonely, scorching wilderness, characterized not by rolling sand dunes but by rocky areas colored in grays, browns, and yellows. Near the coast, limestone produces a dazzling incandescent white glare. Though coastal areas in western Libya have been cultivated since the 1930s, the desert itself sustained little life. Virtually the only vegetation is the hardy camel thorn; an oasis of swaying palm trees is rare. Except for occasional bands of bedouins guiding their camel caravans, only a few creatures survive in this desolation: snails, snakes, rodents, lizards, scorpions, gazelles, hordes of fleas and flies, and the cunning desert fox.

This area posed novel challenges for men at war. Along the sea was a sandy desert plain than ran a few miles inland. To the south lay a high desert plateau strewn with pebbles, rocks, and boulders. Despite inevitable damage to tires, axles, and springs of vehicles, crossing this hostile tableland was possible.

But penetrating northward beyond this stony waste to the coast was difficult. For between the plateau and the sandy shoreline loomed the escarpment—a series of cliffs gradually ascending to five hundred feet, with few passes accessible to tanks and trucks emerging from the Western Desert and headed for the coastal road.

The Western Desert lacked distinctive landmarks. Except for the Via Balbia—the Italian-built highway that skirted the sea—traversing this lonely expanse was similar to sailing an uncharted ocean. Maps were unreliable, and navigation was possible only by sighting the sun, plotting the stars, using the compass, and gauging distances by the odometer. A concentration point for a day's advance by an armored column was not a village or a river, as in Europe, but merely an empty spot in the desert. Fighting on the sand is a lot like fighting at sea. Squadrons of tanks, armored cars, troop carriers, and self-propelled guns roamed the desert like fighting ships ready to destroy the enemy, who could suddenly appear on the horizon. When a combat force sighted its opponent, it maneuvered for position to strike the adversary's flank or rear. Nowhere in the plateau were there defensive lines built near hills, mountains, or cities. Desert combat was fluid, and the principles that governed fighting were speed, surprise, and movement. The Western Desert was the ideal setting in which to try new weapons, devise novel formations of manpower, and test theories of armored warfare. On this sand sea, desert fighting imposed enormous handicaps on soldiers. Commanders had to calculate meticulously their quantities of tanks, weapons, water, fuel, rations, ammunition, and men fit for combat, as they moved their units like pawns and knights over the huge barren board in a deadly game of wits.

Unlike soldiers in combat elsewhere, adversaries on the Western Desert cared relatively little for large territorial gains, because advances deep into enemy ground often wasted precious fuel. Instead, the desert warriors sought to destroy the foe quickly and methodically. A commander could use

RUMANIA

BLACK SEA

BULGARIA

Istanbul

TURKEY

GREECE

Athens

CYPRUS

CRETE

RED SEA

SEA

Derna

Tmimi El Gazala

VIA BALBIA Tobruk

Mechili Gambut Bardia

TRIGH CAPUZZO Collum Sidi Barrani

Benghazi ACROMA PASS Mersa Matruh Alexandria

TRIGH EL ABD CAPUZZO

HALFAYA PASS Fuka El Alamein

Bir Hacheim TELL EL EISA

Bir el Gubi Sidi Omar ALAM EL HALFA

Fort Maddalena

Qattara Depression Port Said

CYRENAICA Suez Canal

Cairo

Mersa Brega Nile

DESERT

EGYPT

Jane L. Reid

the desert for wide maneuvering, or he could go around it by advancing along the coast. But he could do little to modify the hostile environment of this bleak land that depleted his soldiers and crippled his vehicles.

To stay alive in the desert was difficult and uncomfortable; the heat, the cold, the dust, and the sandstorms made life a daily challenge. The blazing sun dehydrated men caught without shade or water, and from morning to dusk it created a shimmering haze that limited visibility. The near-freezing temperatures at night caused men to shiver in the eerie darkness as they waited for daylight, when hordes of insects would return to torment them. Then there was the dust, the unending dust. Thousands of vehicles drove over the desert, followed by marching troops, inevitably stirring up huge clouds of powdery soil. This fog of particles, driven by hot air currents, permeated everything. It seeped through closed lips and eyelids, entered a man's ears and nostrils, caked his face and hair with soot, trickled into rifle barrels, gun breeches, food containers, oil and water filters, and the movable parts of engines. The billowing dust also had tactical consequences, for the rolling clouds of sand over the horizon indicated to the enemy that its foe was on the move.

But the worst discomfort resulted from the feared sandstorms caused by the khamsin, a hot dry wind from the Sahara. A sandstorm started as a little dancing devil shaped like a swirling cone. These spouts of sand gradually merged into huge waves of soil as fierce winds whipped tons of sand into the air to blot out the sun for hours, for several days, or even for a week. When a sandstorm roared its fury, some dauntless leaders might push on, but generally movement ceased. Men crawled under their vehicles or into their tents, covered their heads, and waited for the torture to end. When the sandstorm struck, men huddled for cover, cursed the diabolical desert, and prayed for deliverance from the awesome powers of nature.

Thus the desert determined the character of the campaigns.

The colors of the surroundings were the hues of camouflage. With few dependable roads or trails, armies had to fit their trucks with huge balloon tires and provide special tracks for their armor. The normal daily distance traveled over a bumpy caravan track was six miles. The hostile desert offered little protection against the scorching sun and the chilling night, and both the Afrika Korps and the Eighth Army had to adjust to the environment.

The desert had little water, for rain fell only twice yearly along the coast, and only once every few years inland. Although water could be tapped by drilling deep into the ground and could be sent by pipeline to troops stationed along the Via Balbia, usually every drop of the precious fluid had to be hauled to the soldiers in the desert. Each man received one gallon daily for washing, cooking, and bathing. Soldiers carefully saved the dirty water for the parched radiators of their tanks and trucks. The level of technology of the early 1940s did not enable men to subdue the desert; they could only acclimatize themselves to its daily and seasonal moods.

Newcomers to the desert were impressed with its stark bleakness, its featureless terrain, its monotonous flatness, relieved only occasionally by low ridges and rock formations. In some areas saucerlike depressions dipped below sea level; in most sectors the escarpment rose steadily all the way to the sea, thus inhibiting penetration from the south. Once the men became accustomed to the filmy haze caused by the intense heat on the glaring ground, their visibility improved, and a perceptive soldier could detect more subtle geographic features on the desert, such as folds and curves on its surface or dried stream beds (wadis) deep enough to conceal tanks, artillery, or infantrymen crouching for an assault.

Soldiers crossing the Western Desert found that the ground was usually firm over the plateau, for beneath the shallow carpet of sand was a base of rock and stone, strong enough to support heavy tanks. Sometimes, however, a truck driven by a careless driver would suddenly be mired in a treacherous patch of soft sand. There the vehicle would remain until its crew dug it out or until another truck winched it from the trap. Though the soil base was adequate for tanks and trucks, it was poor cover for nonmotorized units (most of the infantry, the artillery, and engineers), which were not equipped with drills to carve out ditches or tunnels in the rocky soil. With picks and shovels, soldiers dug trenches in the grim shape of coffins. A trench with a tent shelter over it offered some protection from the heat and cold. But, unless they were protected by their own armor or entrenched on a rocky ridge, men on foot were usually helpless before tanks.

The Western Desert was termed "a tactician's paradise and a quartermaster's hell," for the vast expanse offered endless chances for wide flanking probes. Here was a vast emptiness that could swallow a thousand vehicles. They could be virtually invisible to an officer squinting through his binoculars, or even to a pilot flying over the lines. In the desert, unlike in settled areas, only the difficult terrain inhibited the movement of armor. Virtually nothing else stood in the way: no rivers, cities, industrial centers, or farms. Inasmuch as civilians were concentrated in coastal villages, rival armies could fight without being impeded by man-made obstacles. Only the limits on obtaining supplies on the march prevented an adventuresome general from sweeping hundreds of miles around his opponent's flank. The inhibiting factor in such bold raids was the problem of logistics—the theory and practice of provisioning an army. It was extremely difficult to sustain fighting units on the desert for even a week, and in an engagement with the enemy, the amounts of fuel, ammunition and equipment, along with thousands of other items consumed by divisions, required replenishing at double the normal rate.

This relationship between logistics and maneuver was the essence of desert combat. To maintain a precise balance of supply, a desert force traveled like a movable city over the landscape, with its depots moving closely behind. The loss of an oil tanker at sea, the destruction of a truck convoy along the coast, or the failure of an airplane to reach its landing strip could leave armored units stranded in the desert without supplies. Whenever a mechanized army advanced rapidly into enemy territory, its own major bases receded farther and farther to the rear. Few ports were available to help nourish a mobile unit, and the technique of air-dropping supplies was not perfected until later in the war.

The main battlefields lay between El Alamein and El Agheila. Through this region ran the Via Balbia, the struggle for possession of which dominated the pattern of military operations. The armor would emerge from the south, climb, and then penetrate the escarpment to the sea, while the infantry and less mobile forces remained close to the shore, fighting to capture a harbor necessary to mount the next phase of the offensive. As an army advanced, it moved far from its bases and often lost its ability to supply itself, unless it captured the enemy's docks, fuel dumps, and vehicles. Hence, gaining a large chunk of territory was less vital than clinging to a strategic pass, holding an airfield, maintaining a port, retaining the coastal highway, or guarding a desert track in order to prevent an enemy counterattack. Likewise, as the enemy retreated, it neared its own rear bases. Consequently, the enemy became stronger in men and material, while the pursuer became weaker. Supply, therefore, overshadowed all other factors of war, even the environment, the superiority of weapons, and the talents of generals.

These campaigns were the last of the "gentlemen's wars," in which victors treated their captives decently and in accordance with international law concerning prisoners. North Africa was spared the Nazi atrocities typical of German-occupied Europe: the destruction of conquered cities, the obliteration of entire villages, and the extermination of victims in concentration camps. British commandos taken captive by the Afrika Korps were not executed, as commandos were in Hitler's Europe. No SS troops, gestapo (secret police), or special extermination squads served under Rommel. The units in the

Afrika Korps were Wehrmacht (German army). Some of these men supported Hitler; others were indifferent to him; still others felt contempt for him.

The Afrika Korps fought hard, professionally, and chivalrously. The desert was the ideal place for combat, for it was as uncluttered as the ocean. There were no partisan or guerrilla troops to crush, no civilian underground movements to subdue, no refugee problems, and no major difficulties in occupying enemy territory, for the native Arab population was indifferent to the outcome. In some elusive manner, the Western Desert modified what might have been an even more brutal war. The desert set the tempo of the fighting and provided the stage for the struggle over the southern edge of the Mediterranean.

Why Hitler—Germany's führer, or leader—decided to intervene in North Africa is a fascinating tale. His Axis partner, Benito Mussolini, known as Il Duce (the leader), the dictator of fascist Italy, declared war on France and Britain on June 10, 1940. By then victory in Europe was within Hitler's grasp. Only Britain, reeling under successive defeats, remained to be crushed. It appeared that the remaining nations in Europe (Soviet Russia was still a German ally) would topple to the Nazis. Eager to enhance his own prestige and to expand the Italian colonial empire in Africa, on June 28 Mussolini ordered troops to invade Egypt as well as British-held Sudan, Kenya, and Somaliland. With 250,000 troops in Libya and 300,000 in Italian East Africa (Ethiopia, Eritrea, Italian Somaliland), Mussolini expected easy victories over the heavily outnumbered British. While populated centers in England were blackened by tons of Luftwaffe bombs, Mussolini dreamed of conquering the Nile and turning the Mediterranean into a Roman lake once again.

Britain thus faced overwhelming odds on two African fronts, and reinforcements from the Commonwealth nations could not arrive at the Suez Canal for months. The Italian Tenth Army seized posts on the Egyptian border, and the Italian Fourth Army invaded British East Africa, but Mussolini's generals could not boast of victories in either theater of war. Impatient to stride through Cairo as a conquering Caesar, Mussolini ordered the five infantry divisions and the seven tank brigades in Libya under Marshal Rodolfo Graziani to sweep aside the enemy and march to the Nile. To guard Egypt, Britain had only 55,000 troops. To ward off the Italian invasion from Libya—for troops had to be sent to East Africa and to the threatened Middle East—Britain had only one infantry division and one tank brigade.

As the Italians crossed the border, they appeared to be a formidable foe, but British intelligence reports revealed that the supposed fascist power was exaggerated. The Italians were actually poorly prepared for war. Their stocks of ammunition and reserves of artillery had been depleted during the 1930s in the Spanish Civil War, the conquest of Ethiopia, and the annexation of Albania. Most Italian generals were unfamiliar with mechanized warfare, their subordinates were poorly trained for the desert, and their troops were critical of the fascist regime. Theirs was an antiquated army. Many machine guns were rusted, and some artillery dated from World War I. The solid-tired Lancia trucks were often smashed while crossing the rocky plateau, and the flimsy Fiat troop carriers shook to pieces as they traveled over the stony terrain. The pitiful Italian tanks, armed only with short-range cannon and protected by thin plating, were unsuited for combat. Yet the Italians managed to advance slowly from Libya into Egypt. Barely over the frontier, Graziani halted for weeks to consolidate his army, claiming that he was short of equipment and that his troops faced a tough opponent.

Under General Sir Archibald Wavell, commander in chief of the Middle East, the British probed the Italian lines and mounted nightly raids on lonely outposts. Along the coast they tenaciously held a sector and then fell back to establish a new defense. Annoyed by Graziani's endless delays, Mussolini ordered a surge forward of his troops to Alexandria, three hundred miles away, the heart of British naval power in the Middle East. At dawn on September 13, 1940, the second phase of the fascist invasion of Egypt was under way, accompanied by the blare of trumpets and by truckloads of marble monuments constructed to commemorate Italian triumphs on the road to Cairo.

But Graziani stalled again. After reaching Sidi Barrani, only seventy miles inside Egypt, he ordered his divisions to prepare seven camps near the coast. The British desert headquarters was thirty miles eastward at Mersa Matruh, the end of the single-track railroad that ran from Alexandria. Now the relentless law of desert campaigning began to function. The British were close to their rear-line bases, while the Italians were overextended from their main depots at Bardia, Benghazi, and Tripoli. The Via Balbia was constantly shelled by the British navy, and Graziani's desert flank was continually harassed by small, mobile units that terrorized his isolated garrisons. The Italian marshal had violated a basic law of desert strategy: he had foolishly maintained a static front against an aggressive foe.

At Mersa Matruh, Lieutenant General Richard O'Connor, the field commander of the British Western Force (the forerunner of the Eighth Army), waited for reinforcements and for Matilda tanks designed to support infantry assaults. The cumbersome Matilda weighed thirty tons, moved at fifteen miles an hour, fired a two-pound shell that could crack any Italian vehicle, and wore a 78-millimeter metal skin that made the tank almost impenetrable by Italian light artillery fire. While the Italian Tenth prepared a base by constructing airfields, paving roads, laying pipelines, and stocking huge quantities of food, ammunition, and equipment, a small British force prepared a surprise for the invaders.

While Wavell and O'Connor were planning future strategy, two events occurred in the Mediterranean which directly affected the campaign—one, a diplomatic matter; the second, a naval engagement. Jealous of Hitler's string of military exploits, Mussolini sent divisions from Albania to invade western Greece on October 8. The fascist attack confronted the British government with the dilemma: should it meet its treaty obligations of military assistance to Greece or should it forfeit its role as the defender of pro-Allied regimes against Axis aggression? Although Britain had inadequate resources to wage war on the European continent, Prime Minister Winston Churchill assured the Greeks that his country would send troops to the Balkans. The army of Greece fought well and temporarily stemmed the Italian tide, but a German army was poised on its northern border to aid if Mussolini's invasion faltered. Wavell was ordered to prepare an expeditionary force to the Aegean Sea. The second decisive development took place in mid-November when British planes from the aircraft carrier *Illustrious* swooped over Taranto in southern Italy and severely damaged three enemy battleships. This strike reduced the Italian threat to British convoys sailing from Gibraltar to Alexandria and provided the British Royal Navy with additional opportunities to sink unprotected Italian merchant ships scurrying from Sicily to Libya.

Wavell devised a daring scheme to throw Graziani off balance before Germany could intervene in Africa. His intelligence section revealed that the Italians had left a fifteen-mile gap between two of their camps. If a British force could pass undetected through this unguarded opening, he reasoned, it could wreck two, and possibly four, of the enemy encampments. Wavell could spare only 120 tanks and thirty thousand men for O'Connor—the British Seventh Armored Division and the Fourth Indian Infantry Division—against eighty thousand Italian troops stationed in the forward areas. Wavell actually had only limited objectives for the raid: an infantry thrust from Mersa Matruh toward Sidi Barrani, a tank attack on the Italian desert camps and their southern outposts, and the seizure of Bug Bug, twenty miles west of Sidi Barrani.

A veteran of years in the Middle East, O'Connor planned carefully for the raid. He camouflaged his vehicles in desert hues, removed glass windshields to avoid the sun's glint that might catch the eye of wary Italian sentries, studied aerial photographs of the enemy positions, and practiced attacks on sites similar to the enemy encampments. He also had stocks of fuel, supplies, and equipment—enough to sustain his army for five days—stored secretly in the desert. At 1700 hours on December 6, 1940, his small command marched toward the Italian lines. Moving in darkness, O'Connor's men rested and regrouped at dawn, completely exposed to Italian observation planes. One fascist pilot spotted the British columns and reported his findings to Graziani's headquarters, where, incredibly enough, the information was disregarded.

Traveling during a moonless night, British drivers found their trails marked by hurricane lamps, partly covered by cut-out gasoline cans. At 0200 on December 8 the British and Indian units quietly deployed in the rear of Nibeiwa camp, the enemy center of communications. There they waited until sunrise, when the Italians were eating breakfast. Then the lumbering Matildas, armored cars, and Bren gun carriers swarmed into the targets, spitting smoke and flame. The Italians were so stunned that they soon surrendered. Within hours, the British had captured two more camps, for the Italians were unable to coordinate a defense. As the remaining four camps and desert garrisons fell, O'Connor swept onto Sidi Barrani, already under attack by his infantry and under heavy bombardment by the Royal Navy. Even that sturdy fortress, defended by three fascist divisions, toppled to the attackers. By December 12 over thirty thousand dazed Italian captives crowded the road to Mersa Matruh for internment as prisoners of war. On December 13, crashing through all resistance, O'Connor took Bug Bug, the junction where Wavell had originally intended to halt the operation. But O'Connor, realizing that the enemy was demoralized, continued to exploit his advantages. The British force was replenished by huge stockpiles of enemy fuel, foodstuffs, and vehicles. On December 16 the Commonwealth troops advanced to the frontier and captured Sollum and Halfaya Pass. From here, they pushed into Libya itself, storming Fort Capuzzo and Sidi Omar, pressing on like a whirlwind to the port of Bardia.

Humiliated by the defeats, Mussolini replaced Graziani with General Italo Gariboldi and ordered him to defend Bardia. The garrison held 45,000 men and was protected by eighteen miles of defense perimeters. According to traditional theories of war, a general would not attack such a bastion without heavy artillery, shock troops, and additional tank brigades. But O'Connor was not a conventional leader. He had only twenty-three Matildas and twenty light field guns to batter Bardia's walls. Thus, the burden fell to the Sixth Australian Infantry Division (replacing the Fourth Indian, which had been sent to Eritrea), composed of lusty, brawling outdoorsmen who thirsted for a fight. The assault on Bardia was a masterpiece. On January 2, 1941, British Wellington bombers thundered out of the blue to hammer the harbor with missiles. The Royal Navy shelled the wharves, while O'Connor's artillery pounded weak sections of the line. At dawn on January 3 the eager Aussies cut the barbed wire, bridged the anti-tank traps, flung grenades to detonate mines, and cleared a path for the tanks. Under this combined air, sea, and land assault, the city fell. On January 4 the British flag flew over Bardia.

Elated by their good fortune, O'Connor's men paused briefly to enjoy Italian food delicacies and to repair captured enemy vehicles. The Australians painted white kangaroos on the side panels of Italian trucks to indicate the change of ownership. The Seventh Armored Division, calling themselves the "Desert Rats," attached to their tank pennants the symbol of the humble jerboa, a small but agile rat with an amazing ability to survive in the desert.

Tobruk was the next goal, and a great prize it would be. Its docks and warehouses laden with supplies could sustain the British offensive farther westward. Some 140 miles beyond Bardia, Tobruk had to be captured quickly. With the Italians on the run, Churchill ordered Wavell to move to assist the Greeks.

In Berlin, Hitler was furious with the wretched performance of his Axis partner in Greece, North Africa, and East Africa. The führer was also worried about Axis ships, which the Royal Navy was sinking. To assist Mussolini, Hitler sent German fighter and bomber squadrons to Sicily to attack British convoys in the Mediterranean. This decision, ordered one day after Bardia fell, altered the course of the war. The far-ranging Luftwaffe provided protection for Italian vessels and increased the danger to Allied merchantmen. On January 1, for example, German planes sighted a British convoy bound for Malta, escorted by the pride of the British fleet, the *Illustrious*. Wave after wave of Junker 118s punished the carrier, and Stuka dive-bombers peeled off to rip it to pieces. Nearly demolished, the *Illustrious* barely limped to Malta and later managed to reach Alexandria. But the ship was out of action for a year. The damaging of the carrier and the sinking of the entire convoy signaled the beginning of massive air assaults on the key to the eastern Mediterranean—the tiny island of Malta—and gave the Axis air forces temporary control of the skies over North Africa.

After smashing half of the Italian army in North Africa, O'Connor neared Tobruk. Aware that the Germans might send armored units to protect western Libya, O'Connor hastened to conquer the city. The Italians in Tobruk had neither the determination nor the necessary weaponry to resist. Tobruk's defenses were too extensive for the depleted Italian Tenth Army to hold. Again, the fearless Australians cracked the line, the Matildas poured through, and on January 21, the harbor fell to the British. Barely resting, the Desert Rats then raced westward along the coast to Derna, 110 miles west of Tobruk. While his infantry pursued the enemy along the Via Balbia around the bulge of Cyrenaica (Libya's eastern province) to Benghazi, O'Connor had his tank men dash 150 miles over rock-strewn landscape to cut off the retreating Italian army on the coast. Traversing this bone-jarring terrain in their clattering tanks and armored cars, with barely any food or rest, the Seventh Armored Division reached the settlement of Beda Fomm. Only thirty minutes later, plumes of dust along the highway indicated that an Italian convoy from Benghazi was speeding southward to prevent a blockade of the retreating army at that vital bottleneck now held by the Seventh. But the fascists were too late and were unable to penetrate O'Connor's guns and tanks. With the escape route blocked, Italians all the way from Beda Fomm to Benghazi surrendered by the hundreds. By February 7 O'Connor's dynamic campaign was simmering down.

In two months the Western Desert Force had advanced 1,200 miles, captured 130,000 prisoners, 1,000 guns, 400 tanks, countless numbers of trucks, and lost only 2,000 men. At Tripoli, the pride of Mussolini's overseas empire, the battered Italian command was given a rest. Churchill demanded (in what has been regarded as a major strategic blunder) that Wavell stabilize the Libyan front and concentrate on Greece, thereby stripping O'Connor of men, guns, and tanks. Yet Egypt was safe, and British prestige in the Middle East was restored.

Hitler now decided to support his fumbling Axis partner by sending a small force to western Libya to bolster Italian morale. This decision, made on February 11, 1941, marked the birth of the Afrika Korps—a hastily assembled collection of German tanks, motorized units, and shock troops. The Afrika Korps had no desert training; the Germans were unfamiliar with North Africa; and, except for nationality, they had no common bond. But the Afrika Korps was commanded by a tough, ambitious soldier who lusted for glory and who began the first completely mechanized war fought by both sides in World War II. Erwin Rommel would mold the Afrika Korps to reflect his own personality as no other general did with a combat unit in that war. A German general to become famous as the "Desert Fox" was moving onto the scene.

2
ROMMEL

Who was Rommel, and what was unique about him? His background, character, training, and ambitions provide clues to the campaigns that he would wage with the Afrika Korps.

Although in 1939 Rommel was a forty-eight-year-old professional soldier, little evidence in his family background or childhood suggests that he would become a renowned tactician of armored combat and one of the most famous generals of World War II. Unlike most high-ranking German officers, Rommel did not come from an aristocratic background. Instead, his upbringing was typical of the provincial middle class of central Europe. Erwin Johannes Eugen Rommel was born on November 15, 1891, at Heidenheim, in the province of Württemberg, that part of Germany known as Swabia. As a young adult, he retained the tastes and attitudes of the self-reliant, unsophisticated Swabian. Later, Rommel displayed little of the polish or breeding and few of the mannerisms that were associated with the haughty military caste that dominated the Wehrmacht.

In a status-conscious nation, Erwin's grandfather was a schoolmaster and his father a high school principal. His mother, however, was the daughter of a state official, a more prestigious occupation in pre–World War I Germany. During his early education, Erwin showed little scholarly ability, but in his teens he displayed talent in mathematics and athletics.

He became an ardent skier, hiker, and cyclist. Young Erwin was also an expert mechanic. He repaired his own bikes and motorcycles, a pastime that provided fine training for a future field marshal capable of stripping down, overhauling, and reassembling his own tank.

Why he joined the army as a cadet on July 19, 1909, is uncertain. It was apparent, however, that the Swabian was different from his carefree, boisterous classmates. Rommel abstained from smoking and drinking. He was totally dedicated to mastering weapons, acquiring combat skills, drilling his troops, and studying the great military strategists of history.

Rommel earned average grades in the military academy, and in 1912 he was commissioned a second lieutenant in the 126th Württemberg Infantry Regiment. He served briefly in the artillery but soon was back with his rifle unit. The only romantic episode in his early career was his three-year courtship of Lucie Maria Mollin. He married her in 1916, she bore him a son in 1928, and throughout his life he remained totally devoted to her.

Nothing remarkable about the rather dull, but conscientious, young officer who served in various German garrisons appears in the early records. Yet during World War I (1914–1918), Rommel's qualities as a fighter emerged on the battlefields where he consistently displayed courage and imagination. Rommel first saw action on the Western Front in France where he was twice wounded, once trying to bluff three enemy Frenchmen into surrendering, while armed only with an empty rifle. For his bravery, he was awarded the Iron Cross. In October 1915 he became a first lieutenant in a new formation—the Württemberg Mountain Battalion, a commando unit. In 1916, after a year's preparation, this group participated in the invasion of Rumania, where, in numerous skirmishes, and after receiving two more wounds, Rommel again impressed his superiors with his ferocious fighting ability.

His next exploits occurred in the snow-covered Isonzo sector in northern Italy in October 1917. Here he perfected the techniques that he had learned in Rumania. By boldness, by rapid pursuit of the enemy, by quick exploitation of unexpected opportunities (even if it meant disobeying orders), and by pushing his men to the limits of human endurance, he captured ravines, bridges, and a dozen mountain villages. In one incredible day, with only a few hundred men and some machine guns, he captured eight thousand Italian troops, a record for the war by a German officer.

Such feats won Rommel his captaincy and the coveted Pour le Mérite (for valor)—the prized decoration of dazzling blue enamel trimmed in gold on a black and silver ribbon (commonly known as the Blue Max). It was awarded to such distinguished German heroes as the famed killer of the skies, Manfred von Richthofen, the Red Baron. Rommel was fortunate to have missed the long stalemated sieges on the Western Front, characterized by trench warfare and enormous casualties, which haunted the minds of officers who served again in World War II. Rommel's experiences were mainly in mobile operations in southern Europe. There he refined certain principles of war—speed, stealth, fluidity, coordination of weapons, and retention of reserves until the decisive moment to strike—concepts he would later apply to the management of armor.

Germany was defeated by the Allies in November 1918 and under the Treaty of Versailles, which the victorious powers imposed on the embittered nation, the new Weimar Republic of Germany was limited to an army of 100,000 officers and enlisted men. Now twenty-seven years of age, Rommel was picked as one of 4,000 career officers for this small but highly select cadre of professionals who prepared for the next war.

He spent the 1920s as commander of a rifle regiment in Stuttgart where, as hobbies, he assembled automobile engines and dabbled in stamp collecting. He even tried to play the violin. But his favorite amusements were purely physical activities—hiking, running, horseback riding, and especially skiing. Rommel gloried in skiing the steepest slopes he could find. In 1929 he was ordered to the Infantry School in Dresden where, as an expert in small-scale campaigns fought in difficult terrain, he lectured on mountain warfare. Rommel rose slowly in rank, becoming a major in 1933 when he obtained his first independent command—an infantry battalion. Major Rommel had few close links with the influential German nobility, and he even rejected an offer to attend the the army's staff college—the graduate school for future generals. Thus, by toil, study, and total dedication to his work, Rommel won his own promotions. He was that rare individual, a man with a one-track mind, completely dedicated to his profession, with few outside interests, like a certain British officer of his era, Major Bernard Montgomery.

In October 1933 Rommel, then forty-two, was sent to join the new Mountain Battalion, composed of expert skiers. Eager to see if the "old man" could slalom the tricky Bavarian slopes, his younger subordinates invited him to climb a high peak. Ascending it quickly, Rommel led them down the trail in swift descent. He suggested a second ascent and then another rush downward; then came a third exhausting climb, and again Rommel led the race down the mountain. His gasping fellow skiers were duly impressed with the stamina of this robust Swabian.

By October 1935 Rommel, now a lieutenant colonel, was an instructor at the War Academy in Potsdam. The army was expanding, and Rommel was grateful to Adolf Hitler for rearming the nation. Like the general staff of the Wehrmacht, he cautiously supported the Nazi government. In 1935 Rommel and Hitler first met, but no record of their conversation remains. Typical of the German military who held themselves apart from civic affairs, Rommel was uninterested in politics. He privately criticized the führer's propagandist doctrines about the superiority of Teutonic peoples, such as the Germans, over other races and nationalities. Rommel loathed Hitler's infamous storm troopers of the 1930s who tormented

German Jews and opponents of the regime. Rommel's only formal association with the Nazis was a brief period in 1936 as liaison officer between the army and the Hitler Youth, a task from which he soon resigned in distaste. Rommel even refused to join the Nazi party. Yet this ambitious colonel was delighted with Hitler's decision in March 1936 to build a navy and air force, a violation of the Treaty of Versailles that ended World War I.

Eager for medals, promotions, and the smoke of battle, Rommel craved a field command. He reached a large audience with his views on warfare by publishing a highly acclaimed book, *The Infantry Attacks* (1937), which attracted the attention of the führer. As a reward, Rommel, now a full colonel, was appointed to supervise the dictator's military escort at Nazi party rallies at Nuremberg. In October 1938 Hitler selected Rommel to protect him during the annexation of Czechoslovakia's Sudetenland province. Again in 1939 Rommel was at Hitler's side in the German occupation of Austria, another bloodless conquest in defiance of Allied protests. Although Rommel quietly dissociated himself from Nazi propaganda about the inevitable destiny of the Third Reich (as Hitler's regime was termed) to triumph over the rest of Europe, he was impressed by the führer's amazing memory, his exuberant patriotism, and, especially, his courage.

Now fully committed to the Nazis, whether as a party member or not, Rommel was made a major general on August 23, 1939. He became an ardent admirer of the dictator. When Hitler invaded Poland that month to begin World War II (for Britain and France immediately declared war), it was Rommel who was responsible for safeguarding Hitler's life during a tour of the Eastern Front during the one-month campaign. In Poland Rommel observed the techniques of *blitzkrieg*, or lightning war—close cooperation of all military units, reliance on mechanized power, and rapid deployment of Panzer divisions—consisting of tanks, armored cars, self-propelled artillery, and troop carriers—which bypassed points of resistance, cut through enemy communications, and coordinated its thrust with air strikes by the Luftwaffe.

Although he had never even led an armored brigade (about one-third of a division), Rommel asked Hitler for the command of a full division of 436 tanks. On February 15, 1940, the führer gave him the Seventh Panzer Division, then training for the invasion of France. Rommel was fascinated with his 218 clanking metal monsters that toppled trees, smashed walls, and climbed the steepest inclines. Each of his Mark III tanks weighed twenty tons, was nine feet tall, had a five-man crew, was powered by a gasoline engine, and could travel at twenty-five miles an hour in open country. Each was armed with two 7.9-millimeter machine guns and a 50-millimeter cannon that could penetrate Allied armor at nine hundred yards. His division also included support units: a reconnaissance battalion of armored cars, a motorcycle battalion, two regiments of motorized infantry, a battalion of light artillery, a battalion of antiaircraft guns, along with engineers, signalmen, and medical teams. Thus, the Seventh Panzer was virtually a small, self-sustaining army equipped to tackle any military obstacle. Given two months to prepare for action, Rommel plunged into the task of mastering tankcraft. He worked his staff from sunrise to nightfall, made daily runs through forests, and perfected the gunnery and coordination of his armor.

The Seventh Panzer Division was part of the Fifteenth Corps, the armored spearhead for the German Fourth Army that thrust through Belgium and France in May 1940. Although the undersized division was assigned a minor role in the sweep through the Ardennes Forest, Rommel made his command famous by maintaining breakneck speeds, cracking enemy positions, ignoring risks to his flanks, and outdistancing his supply depots. As a comrade in World War I remembered, "Where Rommel is, the front is." The impatient Panzer general was usually in the turret of the lead tank, bullying his subordinates to hurry and ignoring orders from headquarters to wait for support. His division quickly cut through France's Maginot Line on May 16, and it was the first to cross the Meuse River in Belgium. From here, the Seventh thundered on to the Somme River.

Rommel seemed to lead a charmed life. Once, while his infantrymen were toppling, dead and wounded, to the ground from enemy fire, Rommel jumped from his tank and calmly directed an infantry assault on a town. On another occasion, he ran over a smoking battlefield shelled by French gunners to determine why a tank was not functioning. Another time, watching his engineers struggle to build a pontoon bridge over a rain-swollen river, Rommel leaped from his staff car, rushed into the current, and, waist-deep in water, helped his men erect timbers so that tanks could cross.

His division created a narrow corridor, thirty miles long and two miles wide, aimed like a knife at the heart of France. The Seventh was the first to cross the Somme on June 6, and Rommel pushed on to capture the cities of Arras, Amiens, Le Cateau, and then Rouen, only sixty miles from the sea. By June 10, in another mad dash, Rommel had become the first general to reach the Atlantic coast. At Dieppe he had himself photographed crashing his tank into an ocean wall to demonstrate for an enthusiastic audience at home the awesome power of the triumphant Reich. On June 15, still outdistancing his fellow generals, Rommel and his Seventh Panzers captured Cherbourg, France's best deep-water port on the Atlantic.

To the rear, Paris fell to the Germans, and on June 17, Marshal Henri Pétain, head of the provisional French government, signed the armistice. While other Panzer divisions tried to trap the fleeing British expeditionary force at Dunkirk, Rommel was ordered southward. Racing down the coast to the Spanish border, his command covered fifty and sometimes one hundred miles a day. In one incredible test of endurance for men and machines, Rommel's Panzers drove 150 miles in thirty-three hours, establishing still another achievement for the campaign. In his personal blitzkrieg, Rommel lost 40 tanks and 300 men, but he destroyed or captured 450 enemy tanks and vehicles and 300 guns, and trapped 100,000 Allied soldiers, including Scotland's pride—the entire Fifty-first Highland Division. In addition, the Seventh had logged the greatest number of miles of any tank unit. Because of its ability to pounce unexpectedly from the morning fog, the awed French called Rommel's Seventh Panzer the Ghost Division.

During his dazzling performance, Rommel devised several new techniques for battle. He burned entire villages to provide a smoke screen for his tanks; he bypassed strong points of resistance; he maintained complete radio silence by devising map coordinates for the next concentration point; and he probed sites to determine which were defended and which were not. His battle formation was something new. The entire division plowed over the open countryside in a box formation. In front were the Panzers with the armored cars and the shock troops in trucks; then close behind came the artillery and antitank units, followed by the support services and the supply vehicles. Through woods, up hills, over streams, spewing tongues of flame and leaving pillars of smoke in their wake, Rommel's Panzers averaged forty to fifty miles daily. From these experiences, Rommel learned that when confronted by an enemy whose movements were restricted, a mobile unit was decisive. A Panzer division could attack, outflank, encircle, and finally annihilate the foe. His Seventh had demonstrated that what was crucial in modern warfare was not numerical superiority but daring generalship and tactical skill with armor, artillery, and assault troops. The use of a Panzer division, therefore, was based on the fluid, ever-shifting momentum of combat. Rommel insisted that the commander always be at the front, not only to inspire his troops but also to maintain fingertip control of the attack.

Rommel emerged from this campaign a hero and was promoted to lieutenant general in January 1941. But in claiming credit for his exploits, Rommel was arrogant toward some fellow officers. He frequently criticized them for lagging behind the Seventh, although Rommel had ruthlessly expropriated their supplies and spare parts to sustain the momentum of his own advance. However Rommel's own version of how to conduct a blitzkrieg may have dismayed the high command—who considered him a crude, tactless upstart—Hitler was delighted with his favorite field general and awarded him the Knight's Cross, making him the first divisional commander in the French campaign to be so honored.

While the Luftwaffe pounded Britain during the summer and autumn of 1940, Rommel assumed that his division would join the Channel invasion. But Hitler had a special assignment for him—North Africa. Oddly enough, neither Hitler nor his military advisers had contemplated a campaign to recover African colonies lost by Germany in World War I. By 1941 the Wehrmacht possessed no unit trained for tropical combat. No military research had been devoted to conditions in Africa, nor had war games or field exercises ever been held in Germany to simulate problems to be encountered in that continent. But Hitler was worried about the political repercussions in Italy after the successive Italian defeats in Libya, and he intended to demonstrate Axis solidarity. Furthermore, if O'Connor advanced to Tripoli, he could link up with French divisions in Tunisia, Algeria, and Morocco, some of whom were pro-British but hesitant to disobey their orders under the terms of Pétain's peace treaty with Hitler. To bolster Italian resistance in Libya, in mid-January 1941 Hitler appointed Rommel commander of the newly formed Afrika Korps, consisting of only two regiments—the Fifth Light and the Fifth Panzer. By May Rommel was promised a full Panzer division. Hence, the command that was assembled for the emergency consisted entirely of formations designed to fight in Europe, and quite unexpectedly, the German Africa Corps, Deutsches Afrika Korps (DAK), was formed for service in a new theater of war.

Field Marshal Erwin Rommel on the North African front.

In contrast, the British had many years of experience in the desert. During World War I they had learned how to move formations while fighting in Egypt and Palestine against the Turks. During the 1920s the British continued to experiment with desert maneuvers, and in 1936, as a result of the international crisis caused by the Italian invasion of Ethiopia, a Mobile Desert Force was deployed at Mersa Matruh, the first modern desert task force. To this professional knowledge was added the experience of amateur explorers of the Sahara. Some British officers stationed in Cairo, who were fascinated by the desert, made adventurous safaris into unknown areas of the Sudan, Egypt, and Libya.

Thus the DAK should have been at a serious disadvantage when it arrived at Tripoli in early February 1941. But the British squandered their desert inheritance, while Rommel achieved over them the dominance of a desert fox stalking its prey. Under Rommel, the Afrika Korps would revolutionize desert combat and would expand western Libya into a new theater of war for Germany. Rommel's command was not an elite group. True, most of the men were veterans of the Polish and French campaigns, but they had not been selected specifically to fight in the desert. Instead, these soldiers were assembled from various garrisons in Europe in the same manner that a new formation would have been collected to fight in Holland or Norway. The DAK merely typified the training, discipline, and fighting spirit of the Wehrmacht—soldiers confident of their stamina and their skill with weapons.

3
THE FIRST CAMPAIGN

ALTHOUGH HIS force of only two regiments was small, Rommel was delighted with his assignment. In Berlin he studied maps of the North African coast as it ran southeast from Tripoli to Mersa Brega, and then turned northwest along a peninsula dotted with strange names like Agedabia, Benghazi, Derna, and Tobruk. Then the shore resumed a straight line toward Sollum on the Egyptian frontier. South of the thinly populated coast, he noted that the desert stretched unchanging and seemingly limitless. Such vast space, Rommel realized, provided uncluttered room for maneuvers. Tripoli was his starting point for a war of mobility; Cairo and the Nile were very distant possibilities for its conclusion. Though Hitler intended the Afrika Korps to be a mere stone wall for the Italians, Rommel planned to make it a torrent moving under its own laws.

On February 11, 1941, the first German troops disembarked in Tripoli. They were support crews—armorers, quartermasters, supply experts, and water purification teams —units necessary to prepare facilities for a campaign. Within two days, Rommel arrived on a Heinkel 111 bomber. Out stepped this German general from the plane—short, stocky, brusque, bustling, quick in speech, and obviously impatient to begin the great adventure—a man who would quickly impose his style and pattern of command on this new force.

He presented himself to Italy's General Italo Gariboldi, to

whom he was supposedly subordinate. In conversation Rommel soon discovered a defeatist attitude among the Italians, who doubted that their troops could restrain O'Connor from marching farther westward. Ignoring Italian protests that he knew nothing about the terrain, Rommel replied, "It won't take me long to get to know the country. I'll have a look at it from the air this afternoon and report back to the high command this evening." And off flew the amateur pilot in a light plane to observe for himself. From the air, Rommel saw no serious problems in supplying his columns along the coast. Farther inland, he realized, it would be difficult to sustain vehicles because of the terrain, the difficulties of navigation, and the environmental problems.

Peering from his cockpit at the stony plateau below, Rommel wondered if equipment manufactured for use in Europe could function in North Africa. Yet, he was already formulating his theories of desert warfare. As he later wrote, there was actually no distinct type of combat for the desert; only the area of maneuver, like the sea, was different. "When a ship stops, it is located, targeted, and destroyed," he noted. "In the desert, a force must be continually on the move, attacking and probing the enemy. Only the offensive pays. There is no need for a large army, for suitable equipment as motorized as possible should be enough. The desert is wide enough to outflank the enemy and strike him while he is not expecting you." Rommel returned from his flight with only limited data about British strength, but he was convinced that with Italian infantry to support his German units, he could establish a line 250 miles from Tripoli at the coastal village of Sirte.

On February 14 the first German combat unit, the Fifth Light Regiment, arrived at Tripoli led by Colonel Johannes Streich. Hardly were the men off the ship, when each received his tropical kit: an olive green pith helmet (that would soon be discarded for the more comfortable fatigue cap), a sand-colored jacket in the Italian style, and khaki shorts like those worn by the British. The Germans listened to a brief orientation lecture about the climate, and as soon as their vehicles were ready, Rommel hurried them off to the desert. The scarcity of water ahead? Preparations for the diseases of the desert? Special sunglasses? Lotions to protect the skin from the burning sun? Acclimatization to the environment for months before sending troops into combat? Such matters did not concern Rommel, for his men would fight anywhere. They would learn their trade by what Americans now call on-the-job training.

That evening, advanced units of the Fifth Light sped along the Via Balbia in a grueling nonstop race to Sirte. On February 15 the rest of the Fifth hurried to join comrades at the front. Streich reported no enemy resistance at Sirte, and not until February 26, some fifty miles farther on, did a German patrol vehicle fight a running duel with a British armored car. Gambling that the British were retiring, Rommel ordered the Fifth Light onward to El Mugtaa, 150 miles east of Sirte. The next advance would be to El Agheila where the British would probably make a stand. There the shoreline bends northward to Benghazi, another 150 miles along the coast. Already, the Fifth Light was adapting to its environment: digging foxholes in the sand, probing enemy lines, camouflaging guns and vehicles, navigating by the stars, and learning to tolerate the biting cold and pitiless sun.

While the Fifth Panzer Regiment unloaded its tanks at Tripoli in early March, Rommel flew back to Berlin for conferences with Hitler; Field Marshal Walther von Brauchitsch, the commander in chief of the German army; and General Franz Halder, the chief of staff. Rommel found little support there for a quick thrust at the enemy. Hitler—who pinned the Oak Leaves medal on Rommel for his exploits in France—was preoccupied with plans to conquer the Balkans in April and to invade Russia in June. He had no troops to spare for a mere "sideshow." Likewise, Rommel was unsuccessful with his military superiors. He considered von Brauchitsch a fumbling, unimaginative bureaucrat with a limited vision of the enormous opportunities in North Africa. And when Rommel asked Halder for reinforcements and for permission to advance on Benghazi, he infuriated the older general, who ordered Rommel to hold at Sirte and to wait until May for the arrival of the Fifteenth Panzer Division. Only then, Halder insisted, could Rommel begin a cautious advance. Annoyed by the lack of encouragement that he encountered in the high command, Rommel flew back to Libya determined to disobey his instructions and to dislodge the British from Cyrenaica, Libya's eastern province.

Back in Tripoli by March 12, Rommel found his forces in good order. Vehicles were now painted green, tan, and yellow and bore the DAK symbol—the Nazi swastika superimposed on a palm tree. Aware that spies were informing the enemy about the size of his command, the wily Rommel had ordered the construction of dummy vehicles. These fake tanks and phony armored cars were mounted on Fiat or Volkswagen chassis and covered with wood, canvas, and pasteboard to suggest armor plate; they were provided with cut telegraph poles to resemble guns. Left in the staging area outside the city to suggest a large Panzer force, Rommel's "Cardboard Division," duped Royal Air Force pilots who failed to detect the fakes in the glaring sun and swirling dust. To add to the deception, Rommel had his real armor cross and recross the area, stirring up huge clouds of sand and leaving tracks on the desert to indicate that a full Panzer division was training.

On March 14 Rommel had his units parade through the city to boost Italian morale as the Panzers proceeded to El Mugtaa. He displayed his fifty Mark III and Mark IV tanks, seventy Italian light tanks, armored cars, troop carriers, anti-tank guns, field artillery, machine-gun battalions, motorcycle units, and supply and repair vehicles. The DAK was followed by two Italian divisions—the Ariete Armored Division and the Brescia Motorized Infantry—whose destiny would be henceforth locked with that of the Afrika Korps.

Cheered wildly by civilians, Rommel's small force appeared impressive and much larger than it actually was. As the tanks drove through the town's square, their commanders stood straight, saluting Rommel, who watched from the reviewing stand. Watching from the street, Lieutenant Heinz Werner Schmidt watched the vehicles in amazement. "I began to wonder at the extraordinary number of Panzers passing by," he remarked. But then he noticed the reappearance of the same tank with a defective tread. Schmidt realized that Rommel was duping the British by having the column parade through the city, turn at the eastern end of the street, reappear at the western end of town, and pass through again in what seemed like an endless procession of mechanized equipment.

Halting the display for a brief speech, Rommel then addressed his men. "Today we start on a great campaign," he declared. "In front of you is the desert. It is ours—for a great safari." One excited young officer exclaimed, "Heia safari!" meaning "Drive forward!" in the native Bantu of the Sahara. Needing their own battle cry, the DAK repeated the phrase in chorus, and henceforth "Heia safari!" became the war chant of the Afrika Korps.

Just as it had with the Fifth Light some weeks before, the romanticized version of North Africa quickly faded for the Fifth Panzers on the hot dusty drive to the front. They rarely saw Arabs, oases, orange groves, cultivated lands, herds of gazelles, or even camel caravans. Instead they squinted at the bleak yellow plateau, its details obscured by hazy light. As the Italians had warned, it was sheer desolation once a column left the highway. A dry burning wind chapped their faces and dried their tongues; a fine dust pierced them like demonic pinpricks and left uniforms and skin covered with gray grit. At night, tiny fleas emerged from the sand and bit until a man's blood ran, leaving oozing sores that festered for weeks and even months. After a few days the spit-and-polish regulations of the Wehrmacht regarding the properly dressed soldier were ignored. Caps and uniforms were filthy, buttons lost their polish, eyes were reddened by the glare, lips were cracked, and skin was badly sunburned.

Forging ahead in the first tank, Rommel correctly estimated that O'Connor's offensive was over, that the British force was being thinned out, and that it had overextended its logistical support. Although the DAK was intended to be only a blocking force, actually there was little to block. O'Connor was resting in Cairo; the new commander of the Western Desert Force was General Sir Philip Neame, a newcomer to the area. The crack Seventh Armored had been pulled back to Egypt for refitting, to be replaced by the inexperienced Second Armored Division consisting of only one brigade and led into the desert by another novice, General Michael Gambier-Parry. Even the tough Sixth Australian was in Greece, and now two undermanned Australian divisions were on the line. Rommel also learned that enemy squadrons of ships and planes had been transferred to Aegean waters.

Rommel's position was further aided by British errors. Based on reports about Axis forces at Tripoli, Wavell's staff concluded that the Germans would not attack. Wavell's subordinates incorrectly informed him that the coast of Cyrenaica could be defended at the few passes from the escarpment. Thus British guns and armor, it was assumed, could hurl back the Germans. And Churchill, who believed that he was a greater strategist than any of his generals, claimed that the Italians had been thrashed. He was hardly concerned about the DAK, for he was concentrating on the Greek Front.

Just as Rommel suspected, patrolling revealed that the British were retiring to El Agheila, a shabby fortress twenty miles west of El Mugtaa. Here, at dawn on March 25, Rommel lined up his units within full view of the enemy, whom he fooled by moving his Cardboard Division along the enemy flanks. Believing that they were outnumbered by more than three to one in vehicles alone, the Commonwealth troops withdrew without a fight. The DAK now learned for the first time that the supposedly feared Western Desert Force was actually only a paper lion. Now for Mersa Brega.

Flanked by the sea on the north, salt marshes on the south, and situated on sandy hills, Mersa Brega was one of the few natural obstacles on the road to Benghazi. It was a bottle-neck that stood in the way of an Axis advance. Here the British were determined to fight. Ignoring orders from Berlin and Rome not to attack until late May, Rommel decided to move before the village defenses could be made impregnable. He ordered a frontal assault on April 1. From radio inter-ception and aerial photographs, Rommel obtained detailed information about the enemy positions. He sent his infantry and machine gunners to dislodge the British from the north, directed his artillery to pound the enemy lines from the south, and ordered his Panzers to charge right down the highway into the British lines. The enemy guns were well sited, and they should have blown the German armor apart. But Rom-mel was ready with another surprise. By exact timing, he had the Luftwaffe's Junker 111s and Stukas bombard the British artillery and strong points. Yelling "Heia safari!" the infantry charged from the dunes and marshes and captured the town within a few hours. Outwitted and fearful of losing his tanks, Gambier-Parry retreated down the highway to safety. Mersa Brega was a well-defended post, and its capture made the DAK even more confident of its newly developed abilities. Now the Afrika Korps burst over Cyrenaica like a bombshell.

Brushing aside Gariboldi's protests that the expedition was doomed if it maintained its frenzied pace, Rommel pushed the DAK and its Italian divisions another forty-five miles to Agedabia. By April 3 he had thrown out the dazed British Second Armored. On April 4 Beda Fomm fell to the Axis, as the British, like the Italians the previous year, were unable to find coastal footholds to prevent Rommel's flanking attacks from the desert. Delighted with his success, Rommel wrote to his wife that "speed is what matters here." In long desert marches and in short, carefully mounted actions, the DAK was mastering its trade, and it had already recovered a large chunk of Cyrenaica without fighting a major battle.

With his uncanny sense of enemy intentions, Rommel per-ceived that if he could confuse the British about the direction

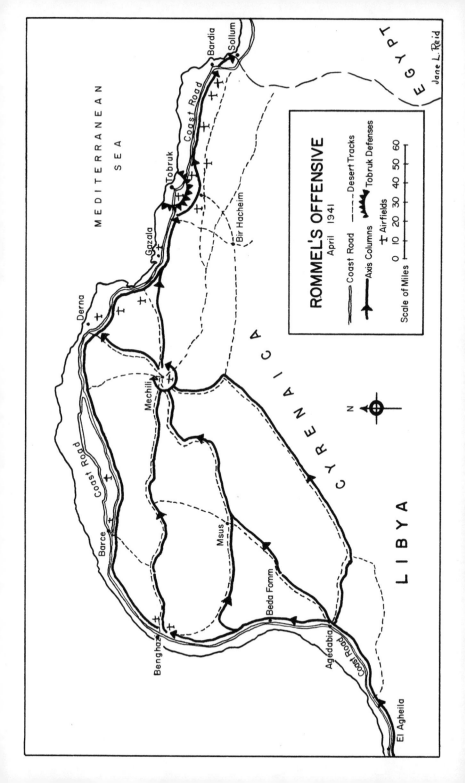

MEDITERRANEAN SEA

EGYPT

Jane L. Reid

LIBYA

CYRENAICA

Sollum
Bardia
Coast Road
Tobruk
Gazala
Derna
Bir Hacheim
Mechili
Barce
Coast Road
Msus
Beda Fomm
Benghazi
Agedabia
Coast Road
El Agheila

N

ROMMEL'S OFFENSIVE
April 1941

Coast Road
Desert Tracks
Axis Columns
Tobruk Defenses
Airfields

Scale of Miles
0 10 20 30 40 50 60

of his attacks, he could force them to evacuate the entire bulge of Cyrenaica, but it was risky. On April 5, without a specific plan, Rommel directed a four-pronged operation across the peninsula to a point four hundred miles away. In complete disregard of military traditions that a general does not split his forces unless he possesses overwhelming odds, Rommel hurried his forces in every eastward direction and confused the enemy by maintaining a whirlwind pace to seize the junctions of Msus, Mechili, Benghazi, Derna, and Tmimi. The northern wing was composed of a mixture of reconnaissance troops and motorized infantry that sped along the coast to Benghazi, bluffing the British into thinking that the Panzers followed close behind. But the real core of Rommel's offensive consisted of three separate columns of tanks and other vehicles that lunged across the uncharted desert to trap the enemy armor at Msus and Mechili. Then the force was to wheel to Derna, Tmimi, and Gazala on the coast.

Rommel had one hundred tanks in operation, but only half of them were the reliable Panzers. Maps of the Cyrenaican bulge were almost useless; some were wrong by as much as twenty miles. For the desert trek, the supply trucks were laden with a six-day supply of fuel, food, water, and ammunition. Rommel realized that he was taking an enormous risk, not only because the DAK was entering unknown land but also because its supplies were still struggling to catch up. Furthermore, most of the units, led by captains and majors who had just arrived from Sicily, had never performed together in battle. Unquestionably, it was a mad dash in a country where tanks needed overhauls after fifteen hundred miles, in contrast to the general repairs given tanks in Europe after five thousand miles. But as Rommel confided to his wife, "I took the risk, against all orders and instructions, because the opportunity was there for the taking."

The motorized troops racing along the Via Balbia toward Benghazi encountered few enemy obstacles, until they reached the outskirts of the city. There the stubbornness of the British defense depended on fighting to the south. For DAK units, the desert was hell. The columns had to plow through layers of sand, pebbles, and rock. Frequently, vehicles bogged down in patches of soft sand, to be hauled out by sweating, straining men, or by quaking trucks. Driving at night, even in moonlight, was maddening, for few landmarks existed, and caravan tracks were barely perceptible without headlights.

Sweltering under a broiling sun (the temperature often reached 122 degrees in the shade), they toiled without rest, creeping forward yard by yard in khamsin, the wind that poured dust into their eyes, ears, nostrils, and mouths, and pushing damaged vehicles through rocky ravines, the men of the Afrika Korps wondered if they could make it. They hoisted trucks out of sand, rolled boulders aside so that vehicles could pass, and strained, grunted, and used sheer muscle power to prevent a tottering truck from falling into a gully. As their trucks pitched and swayed over the bumpy terrain, and as they pushed and hauled vehicles over one ridge after another, the men muttered that this surely must be the last obstacle, the last hill, the last cliff, for they could endure no more. Somehow they managed to drive for miles without rest, with barely a swallow of water or a bit of meat or bread. They even continued to push through sandstorms that raged at over seventy miles an hour. The sand penetrated the filters of engines, and the sun's intensity overheated engine oil; hence there were inevitable delays until the engines cooled. During sandstorms and on moonless nights, units became so scattered that they were sometimes lost. A legend was born on this epic march, a legend that whatever the challenge of nature or man, nothing could stop the Afrika Korps.

Rommel was tireless, driving his men like a tyrant, bullying them to hurry, yelling at officers who lagged behind, screaming at drivers who tried to excuse the breakdown of vehicles, and punishing the poor soldier who fell asleep at the wheel. When Colonel Streich's column of tanks ran out of fuel,

Streich claimed that he needed four days to be supplied. Indignant at the delay, Rommel ordered him to unload all his other vehicles and hurry them back to Agedabia for gas, leaving the Panzer tanks stranded in the desert without fuel. It was a risk that only a Rommel would take, but the formation was replenished within one frenzied day. As Rommel later remarked about such incidents, "One cannot let unique opportunities slip by for the sake of trifles."

Never before had a military force crossed this wasteland, but Rommel was determined to do it. When he was not personally leading a convoy or blaming an officer for losing the trail, he ranged over the area in a Fiesler Storch plane to guide straggling units. Frequently, he landed near stranded columns where he cursed officers for allowing the enemy to escape. As it was difficult to distinguish the hunters from the hunted, Rommel nearly made a costly mistake. Spotting what he assumed were Axis trucks, Rommel landed his plane near the track. But to his surprise as he taxied in, British soldiers with bayonets drawn charged at him and a Bren gun carrier rumbled at top speed toward his plane. Rommel quickly took off in a shower of bullets. His Storch barely managed to bank into a climb as its tail was riddled with gunfire.

After 200 miles of the exhausting desert march, some Axis units under Streich neared Mechili, a crumbling white sandstone garrison that was the headquarters of the British Second Armored Division and the hub from which desert trails radiated eastward and northward. Dismayed that Streich hesitated to assault because he lacked artillery, and that some of his tanks had collapsed in the sand, Rommel immediately ordered the fifteen hundred troops on the scene to attack the six thousand enemy soldiers in Mechili. Eight Panzers appeared over the horizon, stirring up huge spouts of dust, suggesting to the enemy that an entire tank regiment was about to engulf them. The armor plunged ahead and outflanked the camp, while German assault teams threw grenades at the parked enemy tanks and vehicles. Mechili fell on April

6, the Second Armored Division was eliminated as a unit, but most of the Australian infantry managed to escape to Tobruk.

During these actions, Benghazi had also fallen to the DAK. Commonwealth troops streamed along the highway to Tobruk in what they termed "the Benghazi handicap." After another grueling night march, Rommel's armor reached Derna on April 8, but the bulk of the Western Desert Force slipped through his trap. Yet in his swoop at Derna, Rommel had disrupted the enemy nerve center, for his men captured three large command vehicles, built like small buses, that were used for operations, intelligence, and radio transmissions.

Rommel expropriated one of the armor-plated command cars as his own mobile headquarters, and his staff, impressed by its size, promptly dubbed it the "Mammoth." Searching in the captured vehicles for maps, Rommel found a pair of British Perspex goggles designed to protect the eyes from sun and sand. He plucked them up, fixed them to his cap, and grinned, saying, "Legitimate loot, even for a general." But the biggest prize was the capture of three opponents: Neame, Gambier-Parry, and O'Connor himself, who had been re-called from Cairo to assist in the crisis. O'Connor would spend the next three years in a prisoner-of-war camp. Rommel was becoming a famous figure. Henceforth, this relentless German general—standing in the turret of his tank, or sitting sideways on the top of his Mammoth with his cap fixed at a jaunty angle, goggles on his forehead, and the ever-present binoculars strapped around his neck—became world renowned.

Rommel had achieved a series of minor successes with few casualties against a fumbling enemy who blew up their own fuel and supply dumps hours before the sites were endangered and who panicked at the sight of Axis armored cars. By his unexpected strike, Rommel had conquered Cyrenaica in five days, destroyed an armored bridge, demolished several motorized units, and kept the DAK nipping at the heels of the Australians as they hurried toward Tobruk. Tobruk would be

Rommel's next conquest, and with that fortress in his grasp, nothing could prevent the Afrika Korps from advancing to the Egyptian border. With the cooperation of the Luftwaffe and the high command, the Desert Fox, as the British now called him, seemed certain to capture the last British stronghold in Libya. Already by April 9 his motorcycle battalions had raced through the night to cut the road running eastward from Tobruk, while the rest of his men closed in to besiege the city.

Coming as a successor to the German blitzkrieg in France, this runaway conquest in North Africa seemed to confirm the superiority of the Wehrmacht—its men, methods, and equipment. Though the Commonwealth troops would fight hard during forthcoming months, the Afrika Korps possessed the definite psychological advantage of continuing victory. By April 1941 the DAK was winning a reputation as an elite corps.

A remarkable aspect of the DAK, one that has already been noted, was that it was hastily assembled from other regiments in Europe and that its ground troops had little motorized training. The Fifth Light and Fifth Panzer regiments adapted quickly to the environmental conditions of their new home. British units usually required months of training in desert combat techniques. Although the DAK was formed haphazardly, it reached combat efficiency very quickly. The Afrika Korps developed a strong sense of identity as a crack military outfit that was rare in World War II. It happened to the DAK because of its remoteness from Germany and the sense of permanence that came from serving in the same theater of war for years. It developed its own attitudes, behavior, and customs. One should add that the Afrika Korps faced a determined enemy, and to defeat that enemy the Germans had to improve their fighting abilities. Finally, an elite corps achieves distinction not only because of its superior battlefield records but because of the skill and personality of its commander. Rommel was the perfect sym-

A German Panzer Mark III tank with a short 50-millimeter gun.

bol of the German professional soldier. He led at the front, he was fearless, and he drove himself harder than he pushed his men. Rommel unified a diverse collection of soldiers into a distinguished unit because his zeal for perfection in tactics and weaponry was matched by the devotion of his men.

But to place the campaign in proper perspective, one should note that the British Second Armored was unfit for action. Even before Rommel struck, many of its tanks had worn tracks, faulty engines, and a breakdown rate of one tank every ten miles. Furthermore, the British commanders had not developed an efficient logistical system, and their communications network was far inferior to that of the Germans. As a consequence the Western Desert Force lost most of its tanks. On the desert, the tank was the queen of battle. Without armor there was little hope.

Even the German well-gunned, eight-wheeled armored cars were superior to the British models. Of the 150 Panzers (for Rommel was reinforced in late March) that were involved in the fighting, about half were inefficient early models (Mark IIs), but the rest were those capable workhorses, the Mark IIIs and IVs, equipped with the new high-velocity 50-millimeter and 75-millimeter guns with devastating power. Rommel had some 88-millimeter antiaircraft guns, but he was still experimenting with them for use against tanks. True, the Germans had serious supply problems, for they were perennially short of everything. But Rommel was teaching the DAK to overcome such deficiencies, to have units assist their stranded comrades, and to improvise when logistical problems restricted maneuvers. Rommel had bullied the Afrika Korps into accepting several facts: that speed was crucial, that the unit could function on captured gasoline and vehicles, that little time existed for leisurely maintenance, and that regular supplies were virtually nonexistent. Thus, in Cyrenaica, the newborn DAK passed its first test with distinction under its stern schoolmaster. Now for Tobruk and the conquest of Egypt.

4
TOBRUK

THE AFRIKA Korps' campaign to recover all of Libya now centered on Tobruk. Rommel assumed that the British were on the run and that the citadel would easily topple. But instead of "mopping up" fleeing enemy units, Rommel ordered the Fifth Light to remain at Mechili where he expected stiff resistance. When Rommel's staff discovered that Commonwealth troops were retreating toward Tobruk, they tried to inform him immediately.

But where was Rommel? He was somewhere on the fluid, shifting battle line. But in what sector? His staff failed to reach him, and a plane searching for his Mammoth crashed in a storm. By April 5 Mechili had fallen to the Panzers, but Commonwealth ground troops escaped along the Via Balbia. It was typical of Rommel to be so immersed in combat that he was unavailable by normal communications, and, consequently, he could not visualize the scope of a battle.

By April 8 the motorcycle battalion that had bypassed Tobruk to the east rumbled into Bardia. Now Tobruk was completely cut off by land. Rommel quickly dispatched motorized units with artillery to the Egyptian frontier. Then on April 10 Rommel prepared to take Tobruk with a small armored force led by General Heinrich von Prittwitz. Weary from his flight from Rome, Prittwitz was still sleeping at 0600 when Rommel stormed into his tent, demanding to know why the Panzers were not thundering down the highway.

"The British are escaping," Rommel bellowed at the embarrassed aristocrat. Prittwitz jumped into an armored car, signaled his tanks to follow, dashed at top speed down the Via Balbia, and was killed by an exploding mine. It was then clear that the British planned to defend the fortress. If Tobruk could not be plucked like other British garrisons, then Rommel would capture it by assault. For as the Axis force advanced to Egypt, the enemy-held harbor remained a permanent threat to the DAK's flank. Although Tobruk's docks and wharves had limited facilities, its capture would greatly improve Rommel's supply line.

The Desert Fox now launched several probes at Tobruk since he had little knowledge of its defenses. Though weeks would pass before he realized it, the seizure of the fortress was actually beyond the powers of his force. The war of movement now turned into a siege. Although the DAK was mobile and therefore ideally suited for a desert campaign, it was untrained, unprepared, and ill-equipped for this drastic change in the style of fighting. Even though the Italians had constructed Tobruk's defenses in the 1930s, Rommel had poor maps of the area. He lacked aerial photographs of the terrain because the Luftwaffe delayed in sending observation planes. Rommel's troops were weary, and he lacked bombers and heavy artillery to shatter Tobruk's stout defenses. Only a portion of the Fifteenth Panzer Division had appeared, and the rest of its tanks would not arrive until May.

Yet for logistical reasons, Rommel had to conquer Tobruk. It was the only suitable port between Benghazi and Alexandria. Because it controlled twenty miles of the coastal highway, Axis trucks had to detour an additional fifty miles around it to reach the line. The Germans expected the enemy to evacuate, but they encountered something unexpected here —a British determination to cling to the bastion whatever the cost. Furious at the blunders of his desert generals and worried about civilian morale at home, Churchill ordered the fortress to "be held to the death without thought of retirement."

The citadel was sheltered on the north by the sea, on the west by cliffs that dipped sharply to the coast, and on the south and east by a series of slopes twenty miles from the city that ascended gradually to five hundred feet as they neared the defenses. Across this rising plain were *wadis*, slight depressions, and some minor elevations where Rommel hid his equipment, but it was difficult to conceal troop movements during daylight. In addition to its natural barriers, Tobruk was virtually impregnable because of its man-made obstacles. The city was shielded by a semicircle of impediments that ringed the bastion, beginning eight miles eastward, curving in an arc around it, and ending nine miles to the west—a line that extended thirty miles. The defenses consisted of four separate trench systems, deep mine fields, yards and yards of barbed-wire entanglements, fifty concrete pillboxes, dozens of earth and stone blockhouses, broad antitank ditches, and strong points crammed with men armed with rifles, grenades, mortars, and machine guns. To the original Italian defense works, the British had added more barbed wire. They had also enlarged the mine fields, deepened the ditches, and constructed another 150 pillboxes that allowed withering crossfire at intruders.

Behind these obstacles were more trenches, additional barricades, batteries of heavy artillery, and tunnels carved from rock where reserve troops could be concealed. The observation towers of Forts Solaro and Pilastrino to the east, and the hill of King's Cross to the west, in addition to daily Royal Air Force (RAF) flights over enemy positions, provided the defenders with detailed information about Axis movements over the flat terrain that stretched for miles below. The city was well stocked with provisions; its warehouses bulged with supplies; it had artesian well water, a new water distillation plant, and an airfield on which reinforcements landed daily. To Tobruk's wharves the Royal Navy convoyed merchant ships by night in relative safety. Not only did the fortress bristle with weapons and innumerable impediments but it was commanded by General Leslie James Morshead

Australian infantry troops in action.

who led the Ninth Australian Division, probably the toughest infantry division in the Commonwealth.

Even with his back to the sea, Morshead planned an aggressive defense. His artillery continually pounded Axis troops crouching in their foxholes and behind rock piles in the blistering heat. He sent out nightly twenty-man patrols to keep the DAK off balance, and larger units constantly probed Rommel's forward lines after dark to prevent enemy buildups. The Australians were hardy men who quickly adapted to this environment. They were farmers, copper miners, sheepherders, and outdoorsmen from the Outback (Australia's frontier) who were superb marksmen, ferocious in hand-to-hand combat, and far superior to the Germans and Italians in night fighting. If one requirement was needed to mold a new military command like the Afrika Korps into an elite force, it was a contest with a tenacious and dangerous foe. Rommel's men met their match in the Ninth Australian Division.

From Bardia, Axis mobile units rumbled through Fort Capuzzo, only two miles from Egypt. Within three days reconnaissance units held Sollum, the first Egyptian town to fall into German hands, and on April 29 Panzers seized the third key border point, Halfaya Pass. With these posts, Rommel held the strategic entrances to Libya from the east. His tanks and artillery at these points would force British armor to climb the steep escarpment in order to gain access to the Libyan plain. Yet it was dangerous to advance farther, for as long as the Tobruk garrison posed a threat to his flank, Rommel was delayed by a single stubborn division bottled up on the seacoast.

In the spring of 1941 the British were also in severe difficulties elsewhere. True, Wavell reported success in East Africa in repelling Italian invasions of British colonies, but elsewhere the news was grim. On March 2 Bulgaria joined the Axis, and German troops crossed the Danube to the Greek frontier. The Greeks now faced Axis invasions on several fronts. Ignoring Wavell's protests that Commonwealth forces were spread too thinly over Africa and the Middle East, Churchill ordered 58,000 troops from Alexandria and Port Said convoyed to the Aegean to support the crumbling Greek government. Hence, in March, Churchill made a fatal decision in trying to save an ally. In the process, he lost Libya.

In Europe, Panzer divisions invaded Greece on April 6 and entered Yugoslavia on April 14. Under the onslaught of the blitzkrieg, the Greek army surrendered on April 29. The Yugoslav army was beaten in late May. British divisions on the Greek mainland were nearly trapped, but they managed to escape in a heroic evacuation by the Royal Navy. Crete, where the battered troops from the Greek disaster sought refuge, was the next Axis target. In late May, the Germans launched a massive sea and air assault on the island, disembarking amphibious forces on the coast, dropping paratroopers from transport planes, and sending in shock troops by glider.

And the pessimistic reports continued. Malta, the key to the eastern Mediterranean, was savagely pounded by the Luftwaffe. German U-boats roamed the Mediterranean, sinking dozens of Allied vessels laden with equipment for the Western Desert Force. Wavell reported that a French division in Syria sympathetic to the Nazis could assist a German invasion of that country, and oil-rich Iraq, inspired by Axis espionage, could erupt in revolt. It appeared that the entire Mediterranean could be lost. General Francisco Franco, the fascist dictator of Spain, was tempted to join Hitler and Mussolini, to be rewarded with Gibraltar and the French North African colonies. So dangerous was the passage from Gibraltar to Egypt that Allied ships usually followed the much slower but safer route around South Africa's Cape of Good Hope, up through the Indian Ocean to the Red Sea, and then through the Suez Canal.

Yet Wavell played a masterly game on the vast chessboard of the Middle East and East Africa. His commanders crushed revolts in Iraq in May and Syria in June. By early summer they were rounding up shattered Italian armies in Ethiopia. In four months, 250,000 Italian troops had been killed, wounded, or captured. The campaign in East Africa, the first complete British victory in World War II, was over by July.

Meanwhile, Churchill reasoned that even if the Balkans fell to the Axis, Wavell could subdue the trouble spots in the Middle East, and that he could win in East Africa. But the Desert Fox remained the great problem. "Rommel, Rommel, Rommel; that's all I hear is Rommel," growled the prime minister as he restlessly paced his chambers at Number 10 Downing Street in London.

Disregarding the advice of his admirals, Churchill took the enormous risk of sending a convoy of merchant ships and naval vessels through the treacherous Mediterranean. Almost the entire "Tiger" convoy docked at Alexandria on May 12 with 54 Hawker Hurricane fighter planes and 278 tanks. Delighted with the arrival of his "Tiger Cubs," as Churchill called the new cruiser tanks, the prime minister informed Wavell that since the Western Desert Force had been reinforced, no Germans should remain in Cyrenaica by the end of June. Unfortunately the prime minister failed to realize that the Cubs were useless without trained crews, extensive repairs, and refitting.

The fight for Tobruk went on. Rommel studied maps of the terrain, finally sent from Rome, and distributed to his commanders photographs of enemy positions taken by the Luftwaffe. He daily inspected the forward lines and drove impatiently from post to post in his Mammoth, now identified by a large black and white Wehrmacht cross, camouflaged in brown and gray tints, and mounted on large balloon tires. In the early morning and late afternoon when visibility was usually unlimited, Rommel would lie prone on the sand—legs spread apart, cap and goggles pushed back—and peer through his Zeiss binoculars at enemy outposts.

Rommel's unexpected victories in early April and his overextended logistical support had surprised the high command, which was unwilling to risk troops and equipment on a mere African adventure. In Berlin, Halder complained that Rommel had committed the Afrika Korps to an impossible task. Some restraint was needed on the impetuous general, Halder remarked, "to head off this soldier gone stark mad."

As the battle for Tobruk continued under conditions reminiscent of trench warfare, Tobruk acquired a unique significance. After withstanding so many attacks, the fortress symbolized for the Allies sheer courage in defiance of the hated Germans. For the DAK, the seemingly invincible citadel before them mocked their efforts. Someday the "Africans," as Rommel fondly called his men, swore to storm that fortress and to crush the enemy.

Because his force was too small to attack the entire perimeter, Rommel tried to fool the enemy by feinting at some sectors, by selecting one point of entry, and by concentrating his resources there for a breakthrough. The Afrika Korps first attacked in large formations from the south on April 11. The Panzers climbed the slopes, but when they reached the outer wire, they were blasted by an avalanche of artillery shells. Totally exposed on the flat plain, the ground troops behind the armor were mauled by deadly accurate enemy fire. Some Panzers made it to the tank traps but found them too deep and too wide to cross. The first assault was a fiasco.

On April 13 Rommel used a blinding sandstorm as cover for a Panzer regiment attacking with riflemen, machine gunners, and sappers (soldiers who remove enemy mines or lay mines of their own). But again the attack was repulsed by withering tank fire, artillery pounding, the detonation of unsuspected explosives, and the strafing of Hurricanes with cannons sputtering flame from their wings. The German ground troops in the attack lost three-fourths of their strength, and another sixteen of thirty-eight tanks were left as burning wrecks. During the fight, one daring Australian dashed from his trench, singlehandedly charged a Panzer tank and completely immobilized it by ramming a crowbar into its tread sprocket. Here was another demonstration of raw courage heretofore not encountered by the DAK.

Rommel tried on April 14 to rescue riflemen who had been involved in previous assaults and who were now isolated but still fighting behind enemy lines. With only twenty tanks and five hundred men, the Germans managed to make a small breach. But again the losses were high. Only one hundred men survived the fight, and another ten tanks were left as smoldering hulks. On April 16 Rommel thrust from the west with the Italians and personally directed the Ariete Armored Division and the Trento Infantry. But, once more, the British line was barely dented.

After three more efforts were repulsed on April 16 and 17, Rommel detected a decline in troop morale. He encountered opposition to his tactics from high-ranking officers who were stunned by the butchery of their men. Worried about the state of his manpower and the shortage of ammunition, Rommel halted the attacks on April 17—the first major setback to the German army in World War II. The siege had become a stalemate, a crisis of confidence was brewing about Rommel's leadership, and Halder bitterly complained in Berlin that the campaign "was in a mess." It was a harrowing and humiliating experience. The crack infantrymen of the Fifteenth Panzer, for example, baked in the sun all day and froze at night in their tiny slit trenches. They were also bombarded regularly and were maddened by flies week after dreary week.

It was inevitable that the Afrika Korps would compare the stagnant nature of combat at Tobruk to what their fathers had encountered at Verdun, the famous French fortress in World War I, where after enormous casualties, German morale began to crack. At Tobruk there was little glory—only dirt, sand, insects, the blazing sun, and unending thirst. The troops were weary and strained. Noses peeled, lips cracked, skin was blackened. Dysentery and other gastrointestinal diseases were common and incapacitated many troops. The food was wretched and the diet monotonous. The DAK lived on biscuits, cheese, olive oil, and canned sardines. Occasionally, the troops received some black bread and jam. But Germans at home, despite their reputation for efficiency, had blundered. By mistake, potatoes—a German food staple—were not delivered to Africa because of incorrect assumptions in Berlin about dehydration of the vegetable in the heat. German troops were fond of fresh bread, but the quartermaster sent them ovens that could be heated only with wood, which was unavailable in the desert. The troops good-naturedly joked about their meat rations. From Germany came a tinned meat so tough that they termed it *älter Mann* (old man), and from Italy arrived an inedible food in cans labeled AM, which the Germans called *Asinus Mussolini* (Mussolini's ass).

The Italians helped little as front-line troops. Much of their equipment was obsolete or defective. The standard Italian field artillery piece was a copy of the French 75-millimeter gun of World War I. The Italian heavy artillery had a range of only five miles compared with the British guns' range of seven to fifteen miles. Italian-made radios were often inoperative and generally useless in moving vehicles. Their M-13 tank was armed with a mere 25-millimeter machine gun and protected only by thin plates of metal. Hence it was grimly known as the "iron coffin." As a consequence of such undependable weaponry, a standard joke was told in the German ranks: "Why are the Italians such brave soldiers? Because they are willing to go to war with the equipment they have."

Rommel may have agreed with the lowly Italian private, sweltering in his foxhole, who asked: "Why don't you Germans do the fighting, general, and let us Italians build the roads?" Though Rommel barely concealed his contempt for Italian generals, he sympathized with the Italian enlisted men. He frequently inspected their positions, tried to improve their morale, personally decorated many brave Italian riflemen, and often praised the dependable Ariete and Brescia divisions.

Even under the sheer boredom and miserable living conditions during the siege, occasionally there was some excitement. Sometimes a Stuka was shot down by Australian anti-aircraft fire, or a watchful sniper managed to hit an enemy sentry at long range. At night, patrols from both sides might return jubilantly from their latest raids. But the Italians generally had little enthusiasm for combat. With antiquated artillery, paper-thin tanks, incompetent officers, a government, led by the blustering Mussolini, that bred cynicism and contempt, the Italians saw themselves as cannon fodder. They realized that they were poorly led, despised by the Germans, and regarded as a laughingstock by the British. Italian troops, who gradually constituted a growing number in Rommel's command, were needed for their sheer manpower. But the smaller German presence in Libya was vital, for without the DAK, Mussolini's empire in North Africa would crumble. Thus the Axis alliance was an unhappy marriage of wartime convenience, characterized by doubt and distrust.

Dismayed with the pitiful performance of some Italian divisions, Rommel fumed at the inefficiency of their staffs. Not until April 28 did he finally receive a copy of the original defense plan of Tobruk. Only then did he realize why his attacks had failed. The perimeter outside the city was twenty miles long, and it contained more ditches, trenches, mine fields, and strong points than Rommel had suspected. Perhaps a thrust from the east would work, he thought, and possibly reinforcements would arrive from the Balkans. Yet, Rommel was becoming disillusioned. He was worn out, physically and psychologically, from weeks of little sleep, quarrels with his own staff, bickering with the Italians, reports that the Luftwaffe delayed in sending dive-bombers, and the news that U-boats were unable to sink Allied convoys. The complete destruction of his headquarters by a well-aimed enemy shell and the riddling of his Mammoth by a low-flying Hurricane only added to his dismay.

The high command was indifferent to Rommel's difficulties and unwilling to assist him. Compared with the completion of the Balkan campaign in the spring and the preparations for the invasion of Russia in June, Tobruk seemed like a minor affair. Dubious as to whether the Wehrmacht should continue the siege, Halder sent General Friedrich Paulus, his deputy, to investigate the situation. Paulus arrived on April 27 just as Rommel prepared to renew the fight. Although Paulus was appalled at the miserable condition of the troops, he approved of Rommel's plan to assault Hill 209, a slight elevation in the southeast sector. Rommel now had howitzers to lob shells directly at the trenches and pillboxes, and the Luftwaffe assisted with dive-bombers. Surprise was complete, and Hill 209 was captured after a bitter fight. But as the DAK tried to enlarge this bridgehead, Rommel lost half the troops involved in the frustrated assaults. Appalled by the loss of troops, Paulus watched Rommel fail to conquer. Paulus requested him to halt further attacks, and Rommel reluctantly agreed on May 6.

If Tobruk was such a dreary, bloody stalemate, did the DAK learn something from the episode? Unquestionably, the Germans acquired invaluable knowledge about the techniques of static warfare that would benefit them in future campaigns. Troops were schooled in the unfamiliar discipline of trench warfare, known to their fathers but not given high priority in the Wehrmacht's training. German soldiers preferred to fight in daylight, but the barren, open country here required night actions. To match the aggressive Australian Ninth, the Afrika Korps learned how to lay and lift mines, how to patrol offensively and defensively, how to raid outposts, and how to repel attacks—all on moonless nights. The Germans also improved their mortar fire and rifle marksmanship. They detonated mine fields with grenades, concealed their weaponry, and hid during daylight.

Though the DAK was adapting to these circumstances at Tobruk, the basic difficulty was logistics. The Germans were short of every item necessary to support them, and supplies only trickled into Cyrenaica. Rommel needed 30,000 tons of supplies monthly merely to sustain the DAK and another 20,000 tons for stockpiling. The Luftwaffe and the Italian divisions needed an additional 115,000 tons monthly. But Rommel received only 20,000 tons of supplies each month. Some fuel, rations, ammunition, and spare parts arrived by air, but most supplies came by truck convoy from Tripoli, over a thousand miles away, along the coastal road that was constantly bombed and strafed by enemy aircraft. In such a dangerous situation, Paulus urged Rommel to retire westward to Gazala and spend the summer acquiring reinforcements, provisions, and equipment before renewing his offensive.

Indignant with Paulus and the high command for their lack of perception, Rommel had no intention of relaxing his grip on Tobruk. True, fighting on the lines had simmered down, but Rommel wanted the Afrika Korps in championship trim. Instead of waiting at Tobruk until supplies arrived, Rommel gradually removed his mobile units from the area and grouped them on the border to counter a British offensive expected in May. At Sollum, Fort Capuzzo, and Halfaya Pass, Colonel Maximilian von Herff had six thousand Axis troops deployed to blunt enemy efforts to invade Libya. Not content to remain on the defensive, Herff sent raiders into the British lines. Under the blanket of sandstorms, German patrols even hit enemy depots and confiscated British trucks, soon decorated with the insignia of the DAK.

Although the British tanks from the Tiger convoy were still being readied for combat, Wavell could not wait, for Churchill hounded him to attack. On May 15 when Wavell launched his Operation Brevity—a limited thrust designed to capture the German frontier outposts—Rommel was ready. Operation Brevity lived up to its name. It was short, but it was a failure. Commanded by General W. H. E. Gott, one armored brigade and one infantry brigade pushed up the escarpment. After initial successes against Herff's garrisons, Gott's force was decisively repulsed by Rommel's Panzers. The British clung to some ridges, but German armor had recovered Sollum and Fort Capuzzo by May 16, and Halfaya Pass by May 26. Gott lost fifty tanks in this fumbling effort by amateurs against professionals. Operation Brevity was a sorry prelude indeed for the big offensive planned by Wavell for June.

Rommel was unaware that Wavell had received a large shipment of new cruiser tanks on the Tiger convoy. In the murky game of espionage, British intelligence in Cairo had decoded the secret reports that Paulus had sent to Rome about Rommel's pathetic situation at Tobruk. As a consequence, Churchill and his military advisers assumed that the Afrika Korps was stuck in the sand. Regardless of the failure of Operation Brevity, he ordered Wavell to hasten the launching of his offensive.

Yet the British operation was premature. Though the British had an easy superiority over the Italian armor in 1940, they now paid a heavy price for lagging behind the

A German 88-millimeter antitank artillery gun.

Germans in the design and production of standardized, dependable tanks. The British had overworked their equipment in Africa and the Middle East. They were also handicapped by the variety of tanks they used; their armor varied in speed, gun range, and metal-plating. As a consequence, it was difficult for a corps commander of several tank brigades to unify his armor for a mass attack. The pace and performance of the heavy Matilda infantry tanks, for example, kept them tactically apart from the swifter cruiser tanks, the Crusaders.

But the Panzer Mark III and IV were designed from the same model, were standardized before the war, and functioned as a team. And the Germans had another advantage. Since Operation Brevity, the DAK had developed the 88-millimeter antiaircraft gun into an antitank weapon. The 88-millimeter was first used in fixed positions, but later it could be hauled along with mobile units, if provided with wheels. In early June Rommel deployed thirteen 88s and twenty 50s at six points along a curve from Halfaya Pass to Hafid Ridge, six miles south of Capuzzo. He also experimented by keeping four mobile 88s with the moving Fifteenth Panzers. Furthermore, the DAK was reversing the standard theory held by the British that the role of tanks was to hit other tanks (like naval vessels in an engagement at sea), then punch a hole through, penetrate the enemy line, and overrun his rear. The Afrika Korps revised this doctrine by establishing the gun line on which the Panzers would lure the unsuspecting enemy armor. Thus, while British tanks were demolished by antitank guns, the Panzers were relatively free to smash the enemy infantry, artillery, and supply services. Not only had Rommel grasped the offensive potential of armor, but he had also devised the defensive counterpart of enemy armor, somewhat like the sword and shield in ancient battle. Gradually, the 88s would emerge as the decisive weapons in desert combat as they became more mobile and able to function offensively with the maueuvering Panzers, a development that the British were slow to appreciate. Now in fighting trim, well-coordinated, and holding the vital passes into Libya, the DAK prepared for Wavell's next thrust— Operation Battleaxe.

5
BATTLEAXE

BROODING OVER another defeat, Operation Brevity, Churchill almost dismissed Wavell from command for his supposed sluggishness in the Libyan campaign. Wavell claimed that launching another offensive prematurely could be disastrous. He explained to the prime minister that the Cubs were in poor shape. The tanks had to be painted and fitted for the desert. Many had cracked gearboxes, unserviceable tracks, or other mechanical defects. Some lacked basic parts (like sand filters for engine oil), and dozens were inoperative after trial runs. Wavell noted that the Matildas and the Crusaders would be unable to function together and that new crews were unfamiliar with the equipment. He was also deficient in planes because of operations under way in Syria. And RAF squadrons flown in from East Africa to Egypt were unaccustomed to supporting armor. Nevertheless, Churchill demanded that a decisive battle be waged "day after day . . . until you have beaten the life out of General Rommel's army." Risking the prime minister's fury, Wavell delayed Operation Battleaxe until June 15.

Rommel was prepared. With beaverlike energy, the DAK carefully sited and camouflaged the 88- and 50-millimeter guns at key passes and kept the gun barrels low so that the long cylinders would not protrude over the horizon. The Panzer tanks on the line were kept hull down behind slopes or in gullies so that their silhouettes would not be visible to the enemy.

As usual, the basic problem was the shortage of fuel. Rommel had to win quickly and with precision, for he still had to maintain the siege of Tobruk. The Fifteenth Panzer under General Walter Neumann-Silkow was on the frontier with one hundred tanks and eighteen 50-millimeter guns. The Fifth Light with one hundred tanks was in reserve fifty miles to the rear with thirty-six 50s and some older 37-millimeter anti-tank guns. Ariete armor was held at Gazala to check the Tobruk garrison. As a further precaution to restrain the Australians, Rommel ordered a heavy bombardment on the citadel for June 14.

The DAK had another surprise from the attackers. The armor plating of the faster Crusader was 40 millimeters thick; that of the Matilda was 78 millimeters, which made it virtually impenetrable to German antitank shells. One German gunner complained that shells from his weapon "just bounced off the tanks' thick armor. Only a lucky shot on the turret or the tank tracks had a decisive effect." But the DAK now had 88s that could demolish the Matildas at long range. Furthermore, to provide added protection to the Panzers, steel plates were attached to their front and rear to give them an additional 33 millimeters of thickness.

The artillerymen at Halfaya Pass, the anchor of Rommel's defense, first heard the roar of British engines at 0600 on June 15. Confident of success, the Commonwealth units advanced. The attack was in three columns: one along the coast and the northern rim of the escarpment, the second up the central escarpment, and the third on the desert flank. Commanding the attack was General Noel Beresford-Peirse. He directed Major-General Frank Messervy with the Fourth Indian Division, and some Matildas, to push up the shoreline and part of the escarpment. Messervy also led the thrust at the center made by the Fourth Armored Brigade and the British Twenty-second Guards Brigade at Fort Capuzzo, Sollum, and Halfaya

Pass. Wide on the left, aiming at Hafid Ridge was the Seventh Armored Division.

Basically, two British divisions—the Fourth Indian and the Seventh Armored—opposed two German mobile divisions—the Fifth Light and the Fifteenth Panzer. The Commonwealth units had to crash through the Axis defenses or maneuver around them. The number of men, guns, and tanks was about equal in the contest; the RAF had cleared the skies of the Luftwaffe. But the Fifth Light was fifty miles away and could not intervene on the first day of battle. Hence the outcome depended on the damage two British divisions could inflict on the frontier posts, and on the Fifteenth Panzer before the Fifth Light arrived. Both sides were closely matched. Thus, tactics, training, and leadership would decide the outcome.

The attackers made some early gains. On the coast, Messervy won a few miles, but undetected mine fields blew up some Matildas and slowed his advance. On the central escarpment, British artillery became stuck in soft sand, but Messervy's Indian troops captured Capuzzo because the Germans had not positioned antitank guns there. The Indians then moved onto Sollum and Halfaya Pass. Thus, Rommel's quivering line was soon badly dented. But as the Matildas lumbered into Halfaya Pass, they encountered something new. Assuming that they could approach within two or three hundred yards of the enemy, British tank commanders were stunned at the number of mine fields they encountered and at the accuracy of German fire from long distances. Over the radio from Major C. C. Miles came this alarming report: "Good God, they've got large-caliber guns dug in and they're ripping my tanks to pieces."

At Halfaya Pass—commonly known as Hellfire Pass—the Germans used the 88 for the first time as an antitank gun and blasted the Matildas to bits with twenty-pound shells from a mile away. On the escarpment, four Matildas were demolished by exploding mines, and at Hellfire Pass fifteen of the remaining twenty-eight Matildas were destroyed by the long-barreled 88s and the shorter 50-millimeter guns. Hellfire Pass was commanded by Captain Wilhelm Bach, a former Evangelical minister from Mannheim, famous in the DAK as the only officer permitted to use a cane, because of his limp, and for his unmatched skill in siting artillery. Five more times that day, the British stormed Halfaya, but each effort was repulsed by the lethal 88s. The little garrison stood like a defiant Gibraltar against the enemy's armored might. When the attacks ceased by evening, the German gunners celebrated their success by marking white rings around the gun barrels to indicate their number of "kills."

The third column on the desert flank made little progress toward Hafid Ridge until late in the day. Seventh Armored was uncertain about the terrain and advanced almost blindly. It was difficult to identify features in the shimmering haze. Then as the cruisers approached Hafid Ridge, they were hit from three concealed crests. The tanks attacked three times, but they were repulsed. In the last assault, the Crusaders' commanders foolishly charged at some dummy tanks, and they were trapped in the process. Seventh Armored had already lost seventeen tanks. Over the horizon appeared the Fifth Light unexpectedly at dusk just in time to reinforce Hafid and to terminate the action. The day ended with the British controlling Capuzzo and Sollum where they had repulsed the Fifteenth Panzer. But the attackers had been unable to storm Halfaya Pass or Hafid Ridge.

On June 16 Beresford-Peirse kept to his plan. He ordered Messervy to consolidate his grip on Capuzzo and Sollum, and to push on to Bardia, sending the Fourth Armored Brigade to assist the Seventh at Hafid Ridge. The day's fighting was almost a stalemate. The heavily outnumbered Fifteenth Panzer was unable to recover Sollum or Capuzzo, and it was badly hurt in the fighting. At Hafid Ridge, the British Seventh Armored Division spit fire with the Fifth Light in a dozen inconclusive contests that left the area under Axis control. But by now, one-half of the Seventh Armored had been destroyed or severely damaged. Nevertheless, the British generals were still confident that victory would be theirs the following day.

If the British had concentrated their armor on June 16, they could have penetrated the Axis lines, and Rommel would have had to cede the frontier and the siege of Tobruk. But determined to cling to Halfaya Pass, Rommel decided to gamble. He detected that the British generals were too cautious, their command structure weak, their armor and artillery uncoordinated, and Beresford-Peirse was surely no O'Connor. To avoid a renewal of the British attack on June 17, Rommel devised a daring plan. His intelligence learned about the British plan of battle. Instead of keeping his Panzer division separated, at 4:30 A.M. on June 17 he ordered them to break off from their engagements, to link west of Halfaya Pass, and to drive on through that position to create a deep wedge in the enemy formations. Not only did his early counterattack catch the British off guard, but by chance his Panzers crashed right into one hundred British tanks still fueling for the morning's fight. The Fifteenth Panzer was repulsed, but the Fifth Light hit the British rear lines. The British generals panicked. Creagh's armor was so depleted that he could not assist Messervy, and Messervy had to remove his troops. Before Wavell arrived by plane from Cairo, Beresford-Peirse had ordered a withdrawal. By a slender thread, Rommel had won the battle. But as his Panzers were low on fuel and ammunition, he could not exploit the opportunity to pursue the enemy.

The Germans again had performed like professionals against a minor-league team. The new Cruiser tanks did not have the guns, armor plating, or efficiency of the slower Matildas, and many had collapsed on the rocky escarpment. The British persisted in fighting in separate groups and rarely coordinated their tanks, artillery, and infantry as did the Germans. The battle was a turning point for the DAK and seemed to demonstrate Rommel's invincibility. Receiving the news of the latest defeat, Churchill shuddered at the loss of his beloved Cubs. "A most bitter blow," he remarked. Having lost patience with Wavell, Churchill dismissed him, along with three other generals. He replaced Wavell with General Sir Claude Auchinleck. The date was June 22; Hitler's legions were invading Russia.

The British were stunned at their losses of ninety tanks and a thousand men, and they blamed their defeat on the Panzer tanks, not the deadly 88s. As a result of the failure of Operation Battleaxe, the British authorities concluded that their armor was inferior to that of the Germans. It appeared that the Matildas and Crusaders had been repeatedly outgunned. Actually few British tanks had been demolished or severely damaged by the Mark IIIs and IVs. The real killers were the 88s and 50s. Repeatedly, British tank commanders had taken the bait and charged like cavalry at the Panzers, who lured them over slope after slope right into the lethal gun screen. Battleaxe left the British with a long-lasting sense of inferiority about their armor, troops, and generals.

Oddly enough, the architect of their defeat, the wily Desert Fox, was now even more respected by the British forces, not only for outwitting his opponents but also for providing his prisoners with the same rations and medical treatment that his own wounded received. "That bastard Rommel," was the typical Aussie comment, "you've got to hand it to him."

For the DAK, Operation Battleaxe was a clear-cut victory, and the Afrika Korps was proud of the success. For the first time it had functioned as a true Panzer unit against an army of equivalent strength. As Rommel wrote to his wife on June 23: "The joy of the African troops over the latest victory is tremendous." Clearly the DAK was a dangerous fighting organization; this point was demonstrated by their use of 88s, Bach's defense at Halfaya, their superior compiling of intelligence, and the early dawn move to coordinate armor. The skillful fusion of the Fifth Light and the Fifteenth Panzer was a classic example of concentrating armor at a weak enemy point. The Afrika Korps' battle doctrine was sound; its technical skill was improving; its men's faith in their leader was complete.

The men now beamed in delight at the sight of their hero, for clearly the "Africans" had become an elite corps. Unlike the typical German generals who seldom mixed with their troops, Rommel frequently visited his, listening to their complaints, their tales of bravery, and complimenting them for valor. In fact, Rommel, a German, was the most popular general among the Italian soldiers. When he toured the lines, Lieutenant Hermann Aldinger, his aide, wrote that Rommel "feels the need to meet the men who were actually face to face with the enemy, he has to speak to them, then crawl forward to their foxholes and have a chat with them." His mere presence on the line was particularly reassuring to troops as they saw his Volkswagen Kubel bumping along the tracks, or caught sight of his familiar Mammoth bucking and swaying over the sands with its aerial swaying in the breeze.

Although his men had not been selected for their physical endurance, mental ability, or technical skill, Rommel convinced them that they were unique. Major Friedrich Wilhelm von Mellenthin mentioned it: "Between Rommel and his troops, there was that mutual understanding that cannot be explained and analyzed, but which is the gift of the Gods." As if to confirm such impressions, Rommel—who was usually indifferent about the appearance of his unwashed and unshaven men—once addressed a sorry-looking company of soldiers, their skins blackened by the sun, unbathed for weeks, with stubble on their faces. Ordering them to improve their appearance, Rommel exclaimed, "We want young soldiers. We're never going to grow old!" Clearly, Rommel stamped the DAK with his own personality and made a diversified collection of units into his own personal army. With his stamina, his risk-taking, his popularity with the men, he transformed a mixed collection of troops into a tough fighting force. He made the Afrika Korps bold and arrogant. Even when men were captured by the British and embarked as prisoners of war from Port Said, they had the courage to sing a popular German ballad, "We March on England Today."

The enemy regarded Rommel with such awe that it paid him the supreme compliment of targeting him for assassination. From Arab spies, the English learned that Rommel's rear headquarters were at Beda Littoria on the coast. On November 17, 1941, twenty commandos led by Major Geoffrey Keyes emerged at night from a submarine, rowed quietly to the beach, and silently moved through the quiet village. They found the two-story building guarded by only one sentry. Storming the house, the team killed the guard and fired bullets on the first floor. In the bedlam, the electrical generator exploded and the lights flickered out. In the confusion, two Germans jumped down the staircase from above. More shots were fired at random in the darkness. Keyes and two other British officers were killed along with several Germans. The attack was a failure, and the other commandos were soon captured.

But where was Rommel? Ironically, Rommel's headquarters were actually at Gazala, close to the front. Beda Littoria was only a quartermaster's post. In fact, Rommel was not even in Libya that night; he was in Rome. Puzzled by the report of the attempted murder, Rommel was annoyed to learn that the British assumed that he would direct his troops from a comfortable seaside resort two hundred miles from the front.

By now, Rommel had developed a unique style in the desert. He had incredible endurance, especially for a man his age. During battles, Rommel rarely bothered to eat or sleep. Occasionally he napped in his car while being driven to the front, or he slumped over his desk in the Mammoth to rest. Seemingly indifferent to food, he survived for days on bread and sardines, gulping a meal down as he pored over a map or a report. For drink, he carried only a small flask of tea. Virtually tireless, he arose before dawn and expected his officers to be ready when the red Libyan sun appeared in the sky. In terrain devoid of landmarks, he had an amazing sense of direction that perplexed his staff. He frequently astonished them during inspections of the frontier by warning that an enemy patrol was about to appear over the horizon. Invariably, Rommel was correct, even before the telltale dust appeared. He fascinated German civilians at home; they became familiar with the picture of the general who wore a jacket, breeches, boots, goggles, cap pushed back over his forehead, a checkered scarf above his Iron Cross, and the ever-present binoculars. All became known to admiring fans in Germany.

Rommel not only defied traditional military tactics but developed a new style of battle as well. Usually the commander remained behind the lines to direct the course of events by radio, but Rommel reversed the process. He established a fixed operations staff in the rear to keep in touch with him and the Italian divisions; then he drove off to the line. From his forward position, Rommel set the tone and tempo of the attack. With his remarkable sense of a battle's progress, and of the enemy's intentions, he could improvise quickly, order a probe, direct an assault, call for disengagement, or concentrate his armor on an isolated enemy tank brigade. If his car or bus broke down, he would commandeer any available vehicle. Rommel often joined his infantry—crashing through barbed wire, leading tank columns, helping engineers erect platforms over antitank ditches. He never hesitated to push and strain with his driver and aides to haul stranded vehicles out of soft sand. Nothing on the battlefield escaped his attention. He noticed an improperly sited gun, a sector with insufficient mines, tanks with inadequate fuel and ammunition, and outposts with too few men.

On occasion, Rommel was out of contact with his chief of staff for hours and even days. Luckily for him, so ingrained was the German tradition of command training that his operational headquarters often directed the course of battle without Rommel's specific instructions. Fortunately for the DAK, Rommel had excellent subordinates who could easily shift from one specialty to another, or lead a tank brigade in battle. General Alfred Gause, his chief of staff, had remarkable intuition about enemy intentions. Likewise, Colonel Siegfried Westphal, chief of operations; Major Friedrich von Mellenthin, head of intelligence; Colonel Arthur Crüwell; and Colonel Fritz Bayerlein were all talented men. Undoubtedly one reason for the efficiency of the Afrika Korps was the quality of Rommel's subordinates.

During lulls in combat, Rommel answered official correspondence, wrote to his wife and to comrades of World War I, and listened to news broadcasts. Sometimes he showed interest in bits of antiquity found by excited officers—Roman architecture, shards of Egyptian pottery, or Moslem archeological sites—but usually Rommel was bored with such things. He was fascinated by photography, however. He was a skilled cameraman and frequently took shots from a slow-moving Heinkel III of the panorama below. On the ground, he particularly enjoyed taking pictures of British tanks and guns, and especially of prisoners of war. He collected thousands of pictures for a book he intended to write after the war. But as he once told his admiring son, "I cannot photograph my own retreat."

After Operation Battleaxe, Rommel concentrated again on Tobruk. He was certain that Auchinleck would be reinforced and would strike in a few months. So Rommel had to move first. But prudence required certain tactics: keeping the siege under way, retaining a mobile reserve in case of an Australian breakout, and keeping a field force to hold the frontier. But Tobruk was his priority, and his assault force there had to be strong and mobile in order to crack open the perimeter.

During the summer, Rommel prepared for the inevitable autumn–winter campaign. Fresh Italian infantry and motorized divisions arrived. From Germany came the well-equipped Ninety-fifth Light Regiment along with the Thirty-sixth African Regiment, containing many former German members of the French Foreign Legion. At El Duda, a big siege train was established and equipped with nine 210-millimeter howitzers, thirty-eight 150s, and twelve 105-millimeter heavy-artillery guns. The flow of fuel, ammunition, and supplies increased as additional trucks poured down the Via Balbia from Tripoli, and as 3,500 Italians enlarged the Axis bypass outside Tobruk. At Gambut, Rommel's main depot, the DAK enlarged its supply dumps, built airfields, established additional tank and vehicle repair shops, and improved the water supply.

During the summer, the DAK trained with a new intensity, preparing to capture Tobruk. Rommel now had 460 pieces of artillery, additional squadrons of dive-bombers, and an army double the size of his force the previous April. The Luftwaffe flew five hundred sorties monthly over Tobruk, while German artillery hurled a thousand shells daily at the defiant fortress. With such "softening up," Rommel planned to hammer the fortress defenses into oblivion. Then his assault troops, sappers, and engineers would pry open a breach in the southeast for the tanks to hack their way through. The Desert Fox confidently predicted that three days after a record bombardment, his Panzers would rumble onto Tobruk's docks.

Hitler promoted Rommel to the rank of full general, the youngest in the German army. Fearing more Italian control over the DAK, Brauchitsch finally gave Rommel greater power by expanding the Afrika Korps on July 31. Henceforth, these were the elements in Rommel's command: two Panzer divisions, one German infantry division, and the Italian Savona Division. Linked to the DAK, but technically under General Ettore Bastico—who replaced Gariboldi—were two corps. The Twenty-first Corps consisted of four Italian infantry divisions—Trento, Pavia, Brescia, and Bologna. The mobile Twentieth Corps included the Ariete Armored and Trieste divisions. Berlin not only strengthened Rommel's authority but also encouraged him to conquer Egypt.

Even Hitler displayed more interest in North Africa. On June 11 he issued Plan Orient, which provided for a gigantic double-pincers movement to smash the British in Egypt. One arm of the pincers called for the DAK to advance to the Nile. The other arm was composed of German armies directed to advance through the Russian Caucasus, Turkey, and the Middle East. Although the project was temporarily shelved because of the resistance of the Soviet armies that autumn, the existence of the plan showed that Rommel now had greater support. He was expected to capture Tobruk by November. For a few months at least, Rommel's ideas about Africa and those of Hitler converged, accounting for the greater stream of supplies and reinforcements.

In October Hitler ordered the transfer of an entire air force group from Russia to reinforce the single Luftwaffe group based in Sicily. He also transferred twenty U-boats from Atlantic service to Italian bases. Hitler made Field Marshal Albert Kesselring supreme commander, subordinate only to Mussolini, over these air units and over both the German and the Italian navies in the Mediterranean. No longer was Rommel commander of a mere blocking force, as the high command originally intended. To the dismay of Italian generals, Rommel was practically supreme commander of all Axis forces in North Africa.

On the frontier, Rommel never forgot the war of movement, and here, too, the training of the DAK improved. The antitank crews were taught to hold their fire until the last possible moment, so as not to expose their positions. Then, after the 88s had belched their salvos, the 50s and 37s were to fire only when enemy tanks were a few hundred yards away. Here was an improved and coordinated field artillery defense that would again surprise the British.

The tank crews were kept in constant practice. Rommel kept the men of the Fifteenth Panzer Division and the Twenty-first Panzer (formerly the Fifth Light) Division exercising daily to improve coordination with antitank units, heavy artillery, and ground troops. The use of hidden 88s and ambushes baited with dummy tanks in Operation Battleaxe had demonstrated the value of luring the enemy to destruction. But the new technique was to have the 88s and the 50s maneuver among the Panzers so that in a clash the guns could quickly drop into action and enlarge the killing power of the armor. In contrast to the difficulty of firing accurately from moving tanks, the use of self-propelled guns introduced an element of surprise into battle. It provided good sighting from stable platforms, and it hurled armor-piercing shot at greater impact than the 50-millimeter cannon of the Mark III or the 75-millimeter of the Mark IV.

Rommel's general plan was to stiffen border defense in order to check enemy advances toward Bardia, Gambut, and Tobruk. At the frontier passes, therefore, he kept a strong force that would compel British armor to swing wide to the south, where the enemy would consume excess fuel and expose its flank.

But the battle plan was marred by the lack of supplies. Since the summer, supplies had been delayed or sunk as Axis convoys had been pummeled by the RAF and the Royal Navy. From July through October, over 20 percent of Axis ships destined for North Africa had been sunk, and the average monthly tonnage of 70,000 landed for Rommel's force was inadequate. On November 8, for example, an entire Italian convoy was demolished off Tripoli. The supplies landed in November totaled 30,000 tons, and 39,000 tons arrived in December. Deprivation of fuel was bad enough, but how could the DAK fight without ammunition, spare parts, and new equipment? In fact, very few new tanks arrived. But German efficiency in recovering damaged armored vehicles (some of them British), hauling them to repair stations, and refitting them for duty provided Rommel with 250 tanks.

Would the British merely watch from Egypt while Rommel captured Tobruk? As Churchill aptly commented on August 8, "Rommel, Rommel, Rommel. What else matters but beating him?" Yet the Desert Fox ignored the danger of a British offensive. On October 26, he issued orders for an assault on Tobruk for November 20. So confident was Rommel that he could still scare the enemy that he decided to have some fun. Crying, "We're off to Egypt!" he led the Twenty-first Panzers on a midnight raid at an isolated enemy depot. Here the Panzer crews found some prizes—Dodge and Ford trucks from the United States. But the real treat for the hungry men was food—beef from Australia, bacon from England, and canned milk from America.

Rommel returned from his adventure convinced that the British were unprepared for an autumn offensive. But Auchinleck had skillfully concealed his preparations to fool Rommel, and the Desert Fox himself was duped by a German spy in Cairo who unwittingly transmitted to Gambut false information about British preparations to ward off a German invasion of Turkey. Italian intelligence repeatedly warned Rommel that an attack was coming, but Rommel laughed at the news. Rommel's staff even showed him pictures of new enemy depots in the desert, recently constructed airstrips, and an extension of the railroad westward from Mersa Matruh. There were also photographs of South African divisions in training, along with evidence that thousands of vehicles were being concentrated in forward sectors. Yet Rommel refused to believe the clues.

Eager to join his wife in Rome to celebrate his fiftieth birthday and recuperate from the rigors of camp life, Rommel flew to Italy on October 26. He notified his staff that he would return by November 18. In his absence, more data appeared about an enemy buildup. Captured Indian soldiers revealed that a large force was massing, German reconnaissance planes detected long columns of trucks, and mobile patrols reported that enemy divisions were marching toward the frontier. But until the enemy actually struck, Rommel's subordinates hesitated to modify battle plans.

On November 18, just as Rommel returned to Libya, the British Eighth Army (the former Western Desert Force), with

800 tanks and 100,000 men, was nearing the border. Under the veil of darkness, camouflage, and radio silence, the Eighth approached the frontier garrisons. Part of Auchinleck's army was already outflanking the German line to the south at Sidi Omar. At Gambut that evening, Rommel still doubted the information and snapped, "We must not lose our nerve!"

The great Rommel was unaware that Operation Crusader had been under way for an entire day without being detected and that twenty thousand Commonwealth troops were on the frontier. Within hours, the Afrika Korps would be fighting for its life in the bloodiest battle in its history. Operation Crusader would severely test the stamina and skill of the DAK. The Desert Fox had been outfoxed.

6
CRUSADER: THE OPENING MOVES

As THE siege of Tobruk continued, the Afrika Korps and the Eighth Army prepared for the next round of combat by training, and by spying. The opponents sought data about the enemy's positions and strengths. Intelligence compiled from air reconnaissance was useful, but it was often misleading. Both sides concealed equipment, moved regiments by night, erected phony supply dumps, and displayed silhouettes of fake tanks. Interception of radio communication and patrols by light vehicles provided more reliable information about the foe's intentions. Scout cars from both sides continually probed the desert flanks, searching for clues. Sometimes these units unexpectedly encountered each other and fought duels with machine guns in the swirling, choking dust.

Although the Germans sent some raiders on long-range missions into Egypt, the British were more skilled in using teams of men to gather information and to harass rear-line bases in Libya. The most famous of these forces was the Long Range Desert Group. It was composed of thirty adventurers who acclimatized themselves to the desolate plateau like bedouins and who roamed hundreds of miles into enemy country. Moving in small, well-equipped trucks, the group lurked near Axis-controlled roads and tracks, transmitting information about ship arrivals, fuel depots, and truck convoys. The British Special Air Service (SAS), another band of marauders, was actually a small collection of men in cars, trucks, and two light planes. The SAS also gathered intelligence, but its sixty men specialized in quick hit-and-run raids on unprotected enemy installations. The SAS scurried to the Via Balbia to bury mines, attacked small convoys in daylight, and at night blew up supply yards, repair sheds, and aircraft hangars. At lightly guarded Axis airfields, the SAS destroyed over 250 planes parked on the sand. As a result of improved intelligence sources, Auchinleck had ample data about the deployment of the DAK. He even knew the details of Rommel's plans to attack Tobruk on November 20.

Through the summer of 1941, Auchinleck reorganized the Eighth for Operation Crusader, the biggest offensive in the Western Desert. Reinforcements of men, machines, and material were funneled into the Nile Delta. Auchinleck's staff assembled depots close to the border, constructed roads and airfields, prepared secret supply dumps in the desert, concealed concentrations of troops and vehicles, and extended the railroad another seventy-five miles westward from Mersa Matruh. The RAF and the Royal Navy temporarily won air and sea supremacy in the Mediterranean and slashed at Axis vessels. During September about 29 percent of Italian ships destined for North Africa were sunk. In November the figure soared to 63 percent.

In October the Ninth Australian Division was evacuated from Tobruk, to be replaced by the British Seventieth Infantry, the Polish First Brigade, and the Thirty-second Antitank Brigade. Under these favorable developments, it appeared to the impatient Churchill that Auchinleck, like Wavell before him, was stalling. The prime minister hounded his new commander in Cairo with curt instructions to hasten preparations. Auchinleck tactfully answered these criticisms by explaining that the Eighth needed additional training, particularly the Second South African Infantry Division, which was unfamiliar with tanks.

By mid-November, both sides were tiptoeing to action. But

they faced different direction and had different objectives. Rommel prepared to assault Tobruk, and Auchinleck prepared to invade Cyrenaica. As field commander of the Eighth, Auchinleck picked Lieutenant General Sir Alan Gordon Cunningham, a hero of the Ethiopian campaign. Although Cunningham was energetic and confident of victory, he was in poor health and unsuited for desert war. Cunningham had previously commanded only a single division, he was unfamiliar with armored tactics, and he had only two months to prepare for Operation Crusader. Cunningham divided his army into two corps, the Thirteenth and the Thirtieth, each composed of several divisions. The Thirteenth consisted of ground troops and one brigade of tanks. Its commander was Lieutenant General A. R. Goodwin-Austen, a brave but unimaginative veteran of the conflict in East Africa. The leader of the Thirtieth Corps—the armored fist of the Eighth—was Lieutenant General Willoughby Norrie, another poor choice. Indecisive as a leader, Norrie was another newcomer to armor. These were the generals selected to fight Rommel's hardened experts of tank combat.

In material power, the Eighth was well supplied. Cunningham had 800 tanks: 600 on the line, 100 in Tobruk, and 100 in reserve. In addition, he had 600 field guns, 200 antitank guns, 650 planes, 34,000 vehicles, and 118,000 men. The tanks were of four basic types: about 200 infantry tanks (the familiar Matilda and its improved version, the Valentine) and about 600 cruiser tanks—Crusaders and Stuarts. The heavy Matilda was slow and needed refueling after forty miles, but it was protected by 77-millimeter armor plating, and it was mechanically reliable. The lighter and faster Crusader (about twenty miles an hour) was likewise dependable and heavily armored; it fired a two-pound (40mm) shell and had a radius of action of ninety miles. The newly arrived Stuarts from America were swift and had a high-velocity 37-millimeter gun, but they had a limited range of fire, their shells had insufficient power to penetrate steel plating, and they had fre-

A British Stuart tank crossing the desert.

quent breakdowns. The British had unquestioned weapon superiority. But with inept commanders, the Eighth could encounter difficulties in chasing the Desert Fox.

Cunningham encountered the traditional problem of British field commanders trying to coordinate various national groups into one force. The Eighth consisted of Scots, Welshmen, Irishmen, Englishmen, and Indians who had a long tradition of fighting together. But the New Zealanders, Australians, and South Africans (no Canadian units fought in North Africa) had their own customs and mannerisms. Generally, these fiercely independent Commonwealth troops were less well integrated into the Eighth, a factor that delayed cooperation on the battlefield. And there were brigades of Jews, Poles, and Greeks (and later Free French) attached to the Eighth but serving under their own flags and their own officers. These men were intensely protective of their nations' honor.

In contrast, the DAK was more closely unified by German discipline, military training, and the spirit of National Socialism preached by the Nazis. Unlike the British army, the Afrika Korps contained no unit that held itself apart because of class differences. There was only the tension in the DAK that arose from nationality differences between Germans and Italians.

Against the might of the Eighth Army, what did Rommel possess? He had 390 tanks, 70 antitank guns, 200 field guns, 385 planes, and about 10,000 vehicles. His troops numbered 119,000 (65,000 Germans and 54,000 Italians). While the Eighth and the DAK were almost equal in manpower, the Eighth held a two-to-one advantage in tanks and in planes. Though the Afrika Korps had received few replenishments of supplies and equipment after Operation Battleaxe, Rommel made organizational changes that improved its fighting ability. His armored power consisted of the Fifteenth Panzer Division, the Twenty-first Division (the former Fifth Panzer), and the Ninetieth Light Division. Reconnaissance Units Three and Thirty-three each had thirty armored cars. To this core were attached the Twentieth Armored Corps composed of the Ariete Armored and Trieste Motorized divisions. Linked to the DAK but under separate Italian command was the Italian Twenty-first Corps, consisting of four infantry divisions.

Rommel had a variety of tanks. His 146 Italian M13s had a low-velocity 47-millimeter gun and were not a match for any British tank. The DAK had 70 old Mark IIs, infantry tanks armed only with machine guns. The five captured Matildas, now decorated with the Wehrmacht cross, were dependable. Rommel's workhorse was still the Mark III, and he had 135 of these. Mechanically reliable, weighing 20 tons, it carried a short-barreled 50-millimeter gun. To present the enemy with a small target, the Mark III was built close to the ground. Rommel also had 35 new 25-ton Mark IVs, whose stubby 75-millimeter guns fired long-range explosive shells.

But the German tanks were generally not superior in velocity, fire power, or degree of shell penetration to the new British cruisers. Nor did the Mark IIIs and IVs have an advantage in armor covering: the Mark III had 30-millimeter plating, the Crusader 47, and the Stuart 44.

The DAK had enough supplies to mount a quick assault on Tobruk, but not enough for an extended desert conflict that could last for weeks. The Axis units were well positioned between Tobruk and the frontier. Three Italian infantry divisions were at Tobruk. Ariete Armored was at Bir el Gubi to the south, and Trieste Motorized at Bir Hacheim. The heavy artillery faced Tobruk from El Duda and Belhamed, but it could be quickly switched to the south. Southeast of Tobruk was the Fifteenth Panzer under Major General Johannes von Ravenstein, along with the Ninetieth Light. Lieutenant General Ludwig Crüwell, a brilliant strategist, commanded the Twenty-first Panzer Division, which was poised on the Trigh Capuzzo near Bardia. But the only force that actually blocked an offensive along the desert flank was made up of the tiny Reconnaissance Units Three and Thirty-three.

The campaign was fought in gravelly terrain that had few obstacles to impede rapid movement. The major topographical features were the coastal escarpment, the Via Balbia, the northern and southern escarpments, and the main desert tracks of Trigh Capuzzo and Trigh el Abd. Between the northern and southern escarpments ran the Trigh Capuzzo; south of the southern escarpment passed the Trigh el Abd. The Axis bypass road around Tobruk climbed the northern escarpment to the heights of El Duda and Belhamed. Compared with the handicaps encountered in ascending or penetrating the coastal escarpment running from the border to Bardia, both the northern and southern escarpments were easier to cross. Just south of Belhamed, the southern escarpments dipped gradually to a three-mile plateau. Over this gently rising tableland ran the Trigh Capuzzo. On this small plain was the white tomb of Sidi Rezegh, a Moslem prophet.

Near the tomb was an airfield, only ten miles from Tobruk. Although no one had predicted it, Sidi Rezegh became the most contested sector of the fighting.

Operation Crusader began on November 18 as 100,000 men of the Eighth Army advanced into Libya. Cunningham's battle plan called for thrusts at the border garrisons by ground troops and some tanks, timed to coincide with a wide sweep over the desert by armored brigades. The Thirteenth Corps—consisting of the Fourth Indian Infantry Division (three brigades), the Second New Zealand Infantry Division (three brigades), and the First Army Tank Brigade—pushed to the northern frontier. Indian troops were to skirt and then hit from the rear the Axis defenses stretching from Bardia to Sidi Omar. Meanwhile, the New Zealand Division under Brigadier General Bernard Freyberg was to detour around Sidi Omar, march northward to besiege Bardia and assist the Indians in destroying the Savona division on the border. While the Indians were "mopping up" the Italians, Freyberg's soldiers were to advance along the Via Balbia to Tobruk. As the New Zealanders approached, the Tobruk garrison under Lieutenant General R. M. Scobie was to break out and link with the Eighth.

Norrie's Thirtieth Corps was the real strike force, with most of the armor, motorized infantry, field artillery, and antitank guns. The Thirtieth comprised the Fourth Armored Brigade, the Seventh Armored Brigade, the Twenty-second Armored Brigade, the Seventh Support Group, and the First South African Infantry Division. It also contained two other units: the Twenty-second Guards Motorized Brigade protected the rear, and the Second South African Division marched south of the armor to attack Bir el Gubi.

Cunningham had the power and the opportunity to win decisively. As an opening move in this deadly chess game, he sent the Seventh and the Twenty-second Armored to Gabr Saleh, just north of the Trigh el Abd, to tempt Rommel. Cunningham assumed that here the great tank battle would be fought.

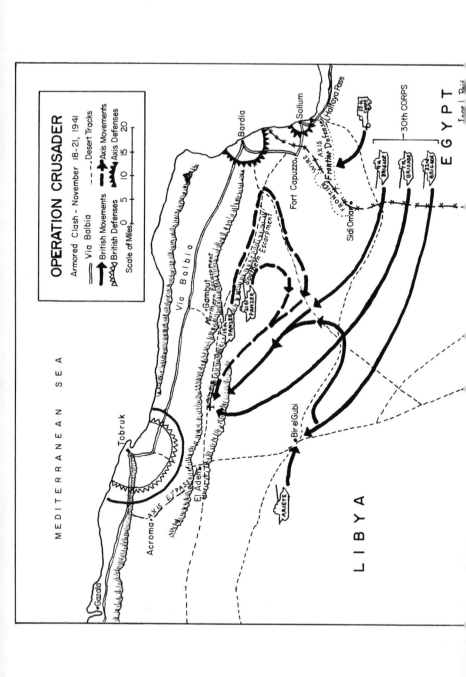

OPERATION CRUSADER

Armored Clash — November 18-21, 1941

— Via Balbia
- - - Desert Tracks
→ British Movements   → Axis Movements
⋀⋀ British Defenses   ⋀⋀ Axis Defenses

Scale of Miles
0   5   10   15   20

MEDITERRANEAN SEA

Tobruk

Gazala

Via Balbia

Via Balbia

Acroma   AXIS BYPASS
El Adem
Northern Escarpment
El Gambut
Southern Escarpment
21st PANZER
15th PANZER

Bir el Gubi

ARIETE

LIBYA

Bardia

Sollum

Fort Capuzzo
WIRE
Frontier Defenses (Halfaya Pass)
AXIS FRONTIER
Sidi Omar

13th CORPS

EGYPT

30th CORPS

4th BRIGADE
7th BRIGADE
22nd BRIGADE

But then he made his first serious mistake. He left a gap of seventy miles between the Thirteenth Corps and the Thirtieth Corps, which was only partially covered by the Fourth Armored. Disregarding Norrie's advice to concentrate his armor for a quick thrust at Sidi Rezegh, Cunningham continued to splinter his tank units. Hardly was the offensive under way when he scattered his armor.

But where was the dreaded armor of the Afrika Korps? Where were those Mark IIIs that the Eighth Army tank crews and artillerymen longed to place within their gun sights? Norrie's commanders spotted only Rommel's armored cars as they rolled over the Trigh and the southern escarpment followed by tanks of the Fourth Armored. Unable to locate enemy armor at Gabr Saleh, Cunningham now split his tank force even more, actually into four disconnected parts. One tank brigade of 135 Matildas was already with the Thirteenth Corps. Part of the Fourth Armored remained at Gabr Saleh while one unit chased enemy armored cars. The Twenty-second Armored went west to Bir el Gubi to tackle Ariete. On November 19, the Seventh Armored headed northwest, as Norrie had urged, to seize Sidi Rezegh.

Even though Operation Crusader had been under way for over a day, Rommel still denied that an enemy offensive threatened his lines. He refused to alert the Fifteenth Panzers, and he ignored suggestions by Crüwell to send the Twenty-first Panzers to probe Gabr Saleh. Part of the problem was Rommel's obsession with Tobruk, but, more important, the weather limited his perspective. Low clouds blanketed the horizon on November 14, and a severe storm on November 15 and 16 concealed the Eighth Army's movements. Not only were Axis motorized patrols delayed, but the Luftwaffe was grounded in pelting rain. Then another storm broke over coastal Libya on November 17, turning Rommel's airfields into quagmires. No Axis aircraft could fly in such conditions on November 18, but RAF airfields in Egypt were barely moistened. As a result, German intelligence failed to detect the massive enemy buildup; mainly because of the weather, but also because of Auchinleck's tight security, excellent camouflage, and deceptive radio messages. Rommel insisted that the Eighth had sent out only a unit to probe his flank. By late November 19 Rommel was finally alert to the danger and moved some armor southward.

The unexpected appearance of the Seventh Armored at Sidi Rezegh airfield aroused the DAK to action. Portions of the Ninetieth Light were rushed to El Duda and to block a tank advance from the east down the Trigh Capuzzo. Luckily for Rommel, the enemy support group with riflemen and artillery was not with the tanks, and the Seventh Armored by itself was too weak to push farther. But the southern escarpment that stretched east of the airfield was wide open for an attack by Norrie's support group the next day, and beyond it lay the exposed northern escarpment and the path to Tobruk.

November 20 was another confusing day of skirmishing and maneuvering. Crüwell's Fifteenth Panzers quickly attacked the Seventh Armored and drove it from the airfield. Here, another twenty-six Stuart tanks were destroyed with few German tank losses. In the meantime, both the Ninetieth Light and the British Support Group clashed on the airfield. The action ended at dusk when Rommel's heavy artillery at Belhamed and El Duda mauled the British ground troops, who were unable to advance beyond the southern escarpment. Yet the Seventh South African Brigade was marching to Sidi Rezegh, and possession of the airfield could again change.

But the main fighting that day occurred near Gabr Saleh. Crüwell spent most of the day on a wild goose chase. Not until dusk did the Fifteenth Panzer Division finally confront a Fourth Armored regiment near the Trigh el Abd. With support from howitzers and 88s, Crüwell's Panzers knocked out another twenty-three Stuarts, losing only four Mark IIIs. Night fell before the Twenty-first Panzers could join the Fifteenth Panzers in the hunt for the rest of the Fourth Armored. But Cunningham should have realized that his plan had backfired. Yet on the evening of November 20, as a result of inaccurate RAF reports and exaggerated messages about dozens of supposedly destroyed Panzers, Cunningham was still certain of victory. He assumed that the battle was proceeding according to schedule. Cairo radio flashed the news to the world that Rommel's army was retreating and that its situation "appeared desperate."

After the fight at Gabr Saleh, the battered Fourth Armored withdrew from the field leaving the Fifteenth Panzer Division in possession. Although the results of this tank action were inconclusive, the DAK remained on the field to recover its damaged tanks, permitting the British to replenish their supplies and reorganize their units in peace. British armor typically retired from the battlefield at dusk and prepared to renew the contest at dawn. But the Germans habitually worked all night to recover their wrecked armor. They sent out trucks to retrieve disabled vehicles, to recover damaged British armor, and to blow up enemy tanks that were beyond repair. About one-half of the tanks damaged in battle could be quickly refitted. Hence occupation of a battlefield at nightfall gave the Afrika Korps a tactical advantage for the next round at dawn.

On November 21 Cunningham expected two separate fights, at Gabr Saleh and at Sidi Rezegh. By now, the British Support Group held portions of the airfield and sections of both the southern and the northern escarpment. Simultaneously, the Tobruk garrison broke out to the south. It cleared enemy mines, demolished Italian outposts, captured a thousand Axis troops, and advanced four thousand yards to the intended linkup at El Duda. Meanwhile the Thirteenth Corps was advancing over the frontier. The Indians had captured Fort Capuzzo and had cut off garrisons at Sollum and Halfaya Pass, while the New Zealanders were threatening Bardia.

Rommel was nearly thrown off balance by these attacks. He could do little that day to assist the Savona division on the border. He was determined, however, to hold the Sidi Rezegh airfield and to prevent the support group from linking with Scobie's troops from Tobruk. First, he reinforced El Duda with Geman shock troops. Then he sited howitzers and 88s at the British Support Group and had his heavy artillery at Belhamed pound the enemy riflemen and a tank regiment creeping along the rim of the northern escarpment. By late afternoon, Rommel had blunted the threat that Scobie and the Thirtieth Corps would connect.

While he concentrated on the escarpment, Rommel ordered Crüwell and Ravenstein to race north to Sidi Rezegh. The tactics of the DAK had been aimless, but Rommel's perception of the shifts in battle are fascinating to study. For as both Panzer divisions approached the airfield, miles ahead of the pursuing Fourth and Twenty-second Armored, their position was decisive. The Panzer divisions raced around the airfield to encircle it and crush the support group.

Then, locating the scattered regiments of the Fourth Armored, the Panzers united and knocked out the enemy brigades one by one. First, the Panzers smashed the isolated Sixth Royal Tank Regiment; then they mauled the Seventh Hussars; finally, Crüwell destroyed the Second Royal Tank Regiment. By the day's end, the British had only ten tanks left near the escarpment. Having demolished the British armor, the Panzers returned to hit the British infantry around the airfield and on the southern escarpment, picking off the field guns of the support group. Infantry of both sides tangled in close fighting with grenades, rifles, and bayonets in savage combat as the tanks roared across the rocky ridges of the escarpment and over the plain.

Too late, Cunningham realized that Rommel had disengaged at Gabr Saleh and that British control of the airfield and his path to Tobruk were threatened unless the Fourth and Twenty-second Armored arrived to assist the hard-pressed Seventh Armored. But, held off by 88s, the Fourth and Twenty-second arrived too late. Though the Seventh Armored was temporarily eliminated and Crüwell held the airfield, Rommel still faced stubborn opposition on the escarpment. Likewise, portions of the Twenty-second Armored and the Second South African Division were advancing to Sidi Rezegh.

On November 22 the contest was renewed in the same sectors. Aware of the threat from the south, Rommel wanted to keep the Panzer divisions together. But Crüwell's communication center had been captured, and he was temporarily out of contact with Rommel. Consequently, he misunderstood Rommel's intentions. He sent the Fifteenth Panzer Division to Belhamed (as Rommel wanted) to blunt the Tobruk breakout, but he led the Twenty-first Panzer Division eastward to Gambut. Crüwell wanted time for his crews to rest and refuel. But, by mistake, he conceded the hard-won airfield to the enemy.

As Sidi Rezegh was being vacated by Crüwell's error, the British had a fine chance to recover it. The Panzer divisions were split, and German infantry was scattered on the escarpments. The Seventh Armored, the Twenty-second Armored, and the remnants of the Fourth Armored were all nearing the airfield from different directions. The Sixth New Zealand Brigade was pressing westward along the Trigh Capuzzo, and the Second South African Division was marching from the south. Just as Cunningham's brigade commanders had victory within their grasp, Rommel pondered the next move.

And here was the turning point of the conflict. Revising his plan four times in three hours because of faulty intelligence, Rommel thinned out his shock troops on the escarpment and deployed them around the airfield. Ordering the Fifteenth and Twenty-first Panzers to return to Sidi Rezegh by devious routes, he managed to position his tanks in time to catch the scattered enemy armor. Ravenstein's Twenty-first Panzers emerged from the north and east and caught the Seventh Armored on its flanks. Then in blinding clouds of dust as the Seventh limped from the field, the Panzers next hit the Twenty-second Armored. By late afternoon, the Fourth Armored finally appeared just as Ravenstein's men ran out of fuel. Unable to appreciate how close they were to victory, Norrie's staff decided to withdraw because of heavy losses.

That fight on November 22 was an epic tangle of tank against tank, gun against tank, fought amid the wreathing smoke, the crump of shells, and the scream of solid shot. The

British again had failed to coordinate their armor, and each time their isolated tank brigades had been outnumbered. As Rommel asked a captured British officer: "What difference does it make if you have two tanks to my one when you spread them out and let me smash them in detail? You presented me with three brigades in succession."

The area around the airfield was a scene of devastation. It was strewn with gutted tanks, overturned trucks, and blackened hulls of burned-out cars. The Libyan plateau was littered by hulks of charred and burning vehicles. The air was rancid with the fumes of oil, rubber, and smoke, and with dust churned up by hundreds of trucks. By evening, the DAK was clearly victorious. Heretofore, the Afrika Korps had a qualitative edge over the Eighth because of its training and discipline. Now this advantage became quantative. The Panzers had 173 tanks functioning against 140 of the battered Thirtieth Corps. By superior tactics, risk, and luck, Rommel had won the day.

And a final turn of the screw came on November 23 as the British were retiring from Sidi Rezegh, expecting that Crüwell's Fifteenth Panzer was far away. But Crüwell had refueled and outflanked the enemy. By 1700 his Panzers were rushing over a shallow ridge to run right into the headquarters of the Fourth Armored, whose men were leisurely reloading ammunition. For the rampaging Mark IIIs, it was like a shooting gallery full of sitting ducks as they knocked out thirty-five Crusaders. The Fourth Armored even lost its communication trucks, and its command headquarters was now another defeated British general strapped in a chair on top of a damaged tank.

In this engagement was Captain Robert Crisp of the Fourth Armored who recalled the incident:

> Twelve hundred yards ahead of me stretched the array of dark brown shapes, 60 or 70 monsters in a solid line abreast coming steadily. . . . The vicious flashes at the end of their gun muzzles stood out in fearful contrast against their camouflage. Behind,

the sky was blood red. I picked up my mike to speak to the gunner: "Cannon. Get cracking!" I heard the first shot go off immediately and watched the tracer sail in a long shallow curve. It hit on one of those dark silhouettes and bounded high into the air. We were too far out of range to do any great damage, but I had to do something. . . . I heard my gunner yell: "I've got one, sir!" and it sounded good to hear his elation and see the smoke curling up from the Mark III and the men bailing out. . . . I had a last desperate search behind me for some sign of rescue and support, and then decided to go. . . . I said . . . "Gunner, cease fire. Driver, advance—turn about—go like hell!"

Then, as for all tank men as they maneuvered during an engagement, came that frantic moment of doubt as Crisp wondered if his vehicle could move. Had a shell pierced the engine? Had a track been shredded to bits? The suspension could be shattered, or the fuel tank could be leaking. Any one of a dozen lurches on the tank's sides during a fight could signal the end of its mobility. "I held my breath," Crisp continued, "and felt the tank heave as the gears engaged. Then the engine seemed to rev high in relief and the tank moved forward."

On November 23, under morning mists and chilling winds, Rommel ordered the Fifteenth Panzers and the Ariete Armored to crush the remainder of Seventh Armored, which was regrouping near Sidi Rezegh. But the New Zealanders had captured Crüwell's base camp, including his decoding, radio transmission, and intelligence sections. With a malfunctioning radio, Crüwell received only part of Rommel's orders. Nevertheless, Crüwell devised his own plan. At early dawn he led the Fifteenth Panzer Division and most of the Twenty-first Panzer Division southward to join Ariete. Then he led his armor east and then ninety degrees north again to confuse the enemy and to strike at the base of the southern escarpment. Here the British were regrouping. The Twenty-second Armored had only twenty-two tanks left, the Seventh Armored was badly mangled, and the support group was low on ammunition. The Fourth Armored had staggered out of action. Nearby were two South African infantry brigades.

At 0800 that morning, Crüwell hit these scattered groups like a thunderbolt. He forced them back into the range of the German infantry, the artillery, and the Fifteenth Panzers, who were dug in at Sidi Rezegh. The British fought hard and sacrificed their Stuarts to save their infantry. At noon, when Ariete arrived, Crüwell decided to forgo tricky maneuvers and to launch a mighty crunch of force. In a tactic unique for the North African campaigns, Crüwell led the Axis armor in two waves of tanks, followed by towed guns and two regiments of troops, traveling by truck, in a mad charge directly at the British armor. Gradually, the pace of the vehicles increased. In one truck was Heinz Werner Schmidt who remembered: "We raced on at a suicidal pace." To encourage their men in this daring tactic, German officers stood erect in their turrets, some killed by the rain of shell fragments. Seemingly oblivious to the hail of explosives around them in the smoke-darkened sky, Crüwell's tanks thundered directly at the enemy, spewing armor-piercing shells and spattering machine-gun bullets.

Crüwell's trap was complete. His Panzers nearly annihilated the Seventh Armored and destroyed half of the First South African Infantry. So complete was the assault that Mark IIIs penetrated to the rim of the southern escarpment and linked to the Panzer infantry. Crüwell's application of brute force at precisely the right time was a unique tactic. The Germans had retained the airfield, cleared most of the escarpment, and prevented the relief of Tobruk. But out of 172 Axis tanks in this battle, known as "Bloody Sunday," 72 were destroyed or badly damaged. The Panzer infantry had suffered heavily, and Ariete was badly hurt. The DAK was not being reinforced. In contrast, although Cunningham was shaken to learn that he had only 40 tanks left on the forward line, his army was constantly replenished with new armor from the delta. Thus, while the Afrika Korps continued to win the contests, the logistical balance was tilting increasingly toward the Eighth Army.

7
CRUSADER: THE CLIMAX

Operation Crusader was actually a series of battles within a larger battle, and after a week it did not conform to any plan. As in most desert brawls fought over huge areas, the deployment of men and machines changed quickly, even before generals were aware of it. To appreciate the blunders and confusion in Crusader, one should know the term "fog of war." By this, military historians mean all those factors relating to weather, staff errors, communication problems, faulty intelligence, misinterpreted signals, and the personalities of commanders that combine to cloud sensible judgments by officers in charge.

Heavy rain reduced visibility, as did frequent dust storms. Hence both sides had the problem of identifying enemy and friendly units. Even with binoculars, it was hard to spot enemy tanks because of camouflage, clouds of dust, shimmering heat waves, and because the opponents used each other's vehicles. Airmen were frequently baffled about whether a column below was a Panzer unit or an Eighth Army brigade. Radios were operated beyond their designated ranges, and the use of low-frequency bands resulted in fading radio transmission at dawn and dusk, just when staff communication was at a peak. Electrical storms could blot out messages for hours. Navigation was particularly difficult as a result of inefficient radios, the feature-less landscape, and inaccuracies of maps. Frequently, after an encounter a German commander had to fire illuminating flares into the sky to show lost comrades where to rendezvous. Likewise, the British shot off Very pistol lights into the dark skies, which by their color and frequency signaled to scattered tank men the concentration area. Thus the peculiarities of desert warfare created uncertainty as to what had already happened and what was now happening simultaneously in several sectors. The dust thrown off by bursting shells, the black, billowing, oily smoke, and the natural desert haze all combined to make tactical control a matter of battle instinct and of personal judgment. Units frequently reported that they could not intervene in a fight because they were unable to discover what was occurring in the dust and smoke drifting over a battlefield.

Clearly, both sides made critical errors in judgment during Crusader. Luckily for Rommel, his Afrika Korps was superbly trained and responded quickly to his orders. Fortunately for Cunningham, he could rely on logistical superiority and on divisional fighting pride. But when opposing generals fail to defeat each other decisively after days of fighting, then victory falls to the side that can withstand the struggle longer. And unless the DAK won a quick victory, it was in danger of bleeding to death without nourishment, while the Eighth was continually being replenished.

Rommel now placed the battle in a new focus. After the triumph of Bloody Sunday, it was time to perform the spectacular and completely demoralize the opponent. He assumed that the Eighth was retreating, that it could not relieve Tobruk or capture Sidi Rezegh. Ignoring Crüwell's advice to obliterate the remaining enemy units on the escarpments, Rommel now directed both Panzer divisions, along with Ariete and Trieste, to push due east, deep into enemy territory. There his force would swoop up supplies along the desert tracks and relieve the pressure on the border garrisons. On November 24, leaving ninety tanks behind, Rommel hurried off on his famous race to the Egyptian border—"the dash to the wire."

At 1040 that morning Rommel himself led the Twenty-first

Panzers on this adventure. Two hours later the Fifteenth Panzer Division followed, trailed by the Italians. If Rommel could pull off this stunt, he could break Crusader, deprive the British of fuel and ammunition, repulse the Fourth Indian Division, and begin his invasion of Egypt. By 1700 Rommel was at the border. Immediately, he dispatched Ravenstein with tanks and infantry to assist Major Bach at Halfaya Pass.

Rommel's gamble stunned the enemy. Most of the Eighth's headquarters and logistical units were located on the Trigh el Abd. The Axis columns caused a stampede among the surprised rear-echelon units. The feared Panzers suddenly emerged from swirling sandstorms, crashed through depots, shoved infantry columns off the track, and shot up helpless truck convoys trying to elude the armor. Brigadier General Robert Clifton, chief engineer of the Thirtieth Corps, remarked that Rommel's tanks drove "almost unopposed, driving everything like sheep . . . completely disrupting our rear organization." German armor even captured the headquarters of the Thirtieth Corps where Cunningham, Norrie, and other generals were conferring. Cunningham barely had time to board a British Blenheim bomber that was chased down the runway by a German truck. Cunningham flew to Cairo where he was hospitalized for nervous fatigue. His replacement was Major General Neil M. Ritchie, Auchinleck's deputy chief of staff. Like Auchinleck and his divisional commanders, Ritchie was determined to continue the battle.

The Eighth did not crack under this stunning blow. Under Ritchie and Auchinleck it quickly recovered its organization. The DAK, meanwhile, was scattered in bits and pieces over the frontier, and its trucks and towed guns were miles behind the armor. Both Panzer divisions ran out of fuel near the border and had to replenish at Bardia. Rommel was incredibly close to a brilliant victory, but again he lacked the resources necessary to push into the heart of the Eighth Army.

Instead, the rampaging Rommel lost his grip. On the night of November 25, he crashed through barbed wire onto Egyptian soil in his Mammoth, expecting his Panzers to follow. But his armor was far behind. Around midnight, Rommel's vehicle broke down in the desert. Rommel, Crüwell, and a dozen top officers spent a cold, sleepless night fifteen miles inside Egypt while cars and trucks of the Fourth Indian Division raced nearby unaware that the Desert Fox was in their midst. The vehicle was repaired by dawn, and Rommel took the wheel, found a gap in the wire, and crashed back into Libya.

Rommel seemed crazed. His orders for November 26 and 27 were pointless. He ordered numerous attacks without reconnaissance. He probed for the enemy in several directions. He revised, reversed, and revoked orders so often that his subordinates were bewildered. What had started as an adventurous gallop to harass the enemy now seemed senseless. When Rommel began to race to Egypt, he had the advantage of several victories. But by November 27 the balance had tipped to Auchinleck.

That evening Rommel finally recovered his senses after hearing the news from El Adem. There, Lieutenant Colonel Westphal, his operations chief, had feared that Rommel's "dash to the wire" was eccentric and that Auchinleck might try to save Tobruk. Westphal was correct. By dawn on November 27, two New Zealand brigades had captured Belhamed as well as most of the northern escarpment and had joined the Tobruk garrison. Now they threatened the southern escarpment.

Westphal was unable to reach his chief by radio that day, and a plane dispatched to Rommel was shot down. But Westphal managed to radio a Panzer regiment that acted as a link to the scattered Axis units. In another demonstration of how a German command post functioned without its general, Westphal ordered the entire DAK back to Sidi Rezegh without waiting for Rommel's approval. The Fox eventually received the information and immediately headed back to the familiar bloody ground of the strategic airfield. On the morning of November 28 the Fifteenth Panzer Division was ready for action, and its target was the New Zealand division.

Rommel gradually prepared the trap. While the Fifteenth Panzers tried to recover the airfield, the Twenty-first Panzers finally pushed over the escarpment, and Ariete appeared to help. Rommel ordered his men to encircle the New Zealanders who had dared to intrude on his domain. On November 30 German artillery mauled enemy troops on the escarpments and pounded the New Zealanders on the airfield. The British were without tank support—the 50-millimeter guns and the 88s held off Ritchie's armor. The Afrika Korps was able to drive the New Zealanders from the field. Even though Ritchie had a superiority of four to one in tanks, he was unable to adapt to Rommel's fluid tactics. On December 1 the jaws of the DAK snapped shut and the isolated Second New Zealand Division was nearly destroyed. Tobruk was again sealed off from rescue, and Rommel was free to deal with the Thirtieth Corps.

Crusader faltered on for another week. Sometimes the battle smoldered; sometimes it erupted brightly. It ebbed and flowed as the participants paused at dusk and resumed the fight at dawn. The DAK still demonstrated its superiority, but by December 2 it was running out of energy. Men were dazed and appeared like sleepwalkers, their faces blackened with mud and gunpowder. Rommel himself was unshaven for a week, caked with dust, and worn out from days without rest. Morale was slipping. Even the fearless tank men of the Twenty-first Panzer Division complained that they were outnumbered.

When Rommel was informed on December 5 that no supplies, reinforcements, or even airplanes would arrive until late December, he decided to cut his losses. He learned that a fresh First Armored Brigade was moving from Egypt and that the Second South African Division was marching to battle. By now, Rommel had only forty tanks in action, and he had to retreat.

With remarkable control and precision, Rommel slowly withdrew. Depots were destroyed, stores at Gambut were removed, and tractors hauled the heavy artillery along the Via Balbia. Rommel managed to extricate his ground troops, thin out his transport, and withdraw the last Italian division from

Tobruk on December 7. Crüwell disengaged at Bir el Gubi on December 8 and covered the rear. If a general cannot be rated a truly distinguished commander until he has withstood the tests of defeat and retreat, then the same applies to an army. The Afrika Korps lost many men, officers, and much equipment. But morale remained high, even in pelting rain, under constant RAF strafing, and on empty stomachs. The DAK still had the will to fight. During the retreat to Gazala, some forty miles from Tobruk, it mined roads, fought rear-guard actions, protected stragglers, and blunted punches on its flanks by the Twenty-second Armored Division. Thus, even while being pursued, the Germans could stand, hold, snap back, and inflict numbing wounds on their tormentors.

By December 11 the Afrika Korps held a defensive line at Gazala. The so-called Gazala Line was actually a flimsy posi-

Rommel's men repairing equipment.

tion with many gaps. From the sea at Gazala, it ran ten miles south to the ridge of Alam Hamza. Realizing that his position at Gazala was untenable, Rommel retired down the coast to Benghazi on December 17. Here his famished men replenished their food supplies and then evacuated the city. One dauntless German sergeant wrote a message to the Eighth Army on the wall of a deserted house: "Back soon—in three months!" By December 23 the DAK was safe at Beda Fomm. Rommel had retreated three hundred miles in a month, he had kept his command intact and had inflicted severe wounds on his pursuers. But Rommel was bitterly humiliated by his first defeat. Some of his finest troops were dead, severely wounded, or captured. His once-proud Panzers were only a skeleton force, and the Afrika Korps seemed on the verge of being driven back to Tripoli.

Not only had Cyrenaica been lost, but the frontier posts soon toppled. Bardia and Sollum fell on January 4, 1942, and defiant Halfaya Pass finally surrendered on January 17. Rommel lost 320 tanks and 38,000 men in Operation Crusader. In contrast, the Eighth Army lost 378 tanks and 17,000 troops. Auchinleck had saved Tobruk, cleared Cyrenaica, captured airfields, and destroyed German armor. His army seemed poised to wipe out the supposedly beaten Afrika Korps, as Churchill announced with delight in the British House of Commons.

Though Crusader was a British victory, it was not a major triumph. The British commanders had blundered too often, and they had wasted soldiers and equipment. Crusader seemed like an endless series of surprises and muddles. Yet the British had gained valuable experience, and they had a clearer picture of what could be accomplished on the desert.

In perspective, the performance of the DAK in Crusader was remarkable. It lost the battle only because of logistics. Between July and October the monthly average of military cargoes landed in Libya was 72,000 tons, just enough to sustain Rommel's command. But in November the supply tonnage was only 30,000 and in December 39,000. No army, not even one as tough as the Afrika Korps, could withstand a prolonged conflict choked by lack of fuel and ammunition. The DAK actually emerged from the ordeal unbroken in spirit. True, Rommel and Crüwell made some grave tactical errors. But Rommel had a well-drilled instrument that responded quickly. And luckily for the Germans, the Eighth Army was poorly led. After logistics, leadership was the second key to Crusader. The British had not found a Rommel of their own.

North Africa now became more vital in the strategy of the German high command. On January 2, two thousand tons of precious fuel reached Tripoli in a concerted effort to reinforce the DAK. By January 12 another Luftwaffe air group had reinforced squadrons based in southern Italy to neutralize the Malta-based planes and ships that had destroyed 75 percent of Rommel's cargoes in November.

But the most significant event had occurred on December 7, 1941, when the Japanese navy and air force bombed Pearl Harbor in Hawaii. This brought the United States into the war against the Axis powers. America's manpower, its full industrial might, and its technological know-how were now fully committed to the Allied cause. In the Far East the Japanese were sweeping over southeast Asia. They conquered the Philippines and invaded Burma and Malaya. By controlling numerous islands in the South Pacific, the Japanese became a threat to Australia and New Zealand. Even India seemed in danger. As a result, the Japanese menace to the Commonwealth in the Pacific and Indian oceans forced Auchinleck to detach units from the Middle East for service in Burma and New Guinea. Resources for Egypt were now diverted to stem the tide of Japanese conquest. Control of Tripoli faded as a major objective, just as the Greek crisis had intervened in 1941 to prevent O'Connor's complete victory.

Meanwhile Rommel made two quick gains. Just before Benghazi was evacuated, an Italian ship unloaded twenty-two tanks for the Fifteenth Panzers. On December 23 another vessel docked at Tripoli with twenty-three tanks for the Twenty-first Panzer Division. This new armor was particularly valuable in Rommel's planning, because British intelligence in Cairo had failed to detect the reinforcements to the DAK. On December 28 and 30 skirmishes between the Panzers and the Twenty-second Armored resulted in losses of sixty of the ninety British tanks in the fight. Clearly, the Afrika Korps was back in business.

8
LIFE IN THE DESERT

THROUGH THE long months of campaigning, how did the Afrika Korps and the Eighth Army adjust to the desert environment? Soldiers on both sides commented about their unique experiences. They wrote about the scorching heat of day, the chilling winds of night, the billowing sandstorms, the swarms of loathsome insects, the spectacular sunsets, and the heavens filled with stars.

The intense heat, the scarcity of water, the monotony of the food rations made the grueling life a challenge. Although the Eighth was far better supplied with water and provisions than was the DAK, both sides shared the same discomforts. Because of dietary deficiencies, jaundice was common. Heat stroke was frequent. Intestinal disorders such as dysentery created long lines at sick call. The worst ailments were desert sores resulting from fleabites, the tearing of flesh on prickly camel-thorn bush, and cuts suffered while digging entrenchments, cleaning weapons, and handling barbed wire. Sand penetrated these minor wounds and enlarged them, creating running sores that festered for months. Many servicemen spent months with gauze wrapped around their arms or legs, for healing was a very slow process. Auchinleck correctly termed the desert as the place of "blood, sweat, and thirst." And he could have added "desert diseases."

Even metal, exposed to the sun, was dangerous. Soldiers

frequently burned themselves on hot gun barrels or armor plating. The temperature on the surface of an immobile tank could rise to 160 degrees. Sometimes men tried to fry eggs on the armor, but such cooking was really a stunt. Always the publicity-seeker, Rommel ordered cameramen to photograph eggs sizzling on a Mark III to impress his fans at home. The heat was not quite intense enough, however, so Rommel had an acetylene torch applied to the metal. The photographers soon had pictures of eggs cooking in the blazing sun.

The desert warriors used various devices necessary for the desert. To protect themselves from swarms of flies that descended on their eyes, lips, and nostrils they covered their head and shoulders with thin netting. To ward off the streams of powdery sand, mobile teams wore tight-fitting goggles. Ground troops caught in a khamsin, a hot south wind, wore cloth masks and even gas masks to protect their faces from the pelting sand. Men knew that a slit trench was useful to provide some warmth from the biting night wind.

Water was the main worry for the Afrika Korps. The Eighth had far more, thanks to its extensive system of pipelines. Sometimes rainwater was available in desert cisterns where soldiers took a rare bath. But inasmuch as rain was rare, cisterns were usually dry. Troops regarded water as the most precious commodity in the desert. When the DAK attacked the Gazala Line in the summer of 1942, it carried water for only four days: one gallon daily for each man, one for each truck, and four for each tank. If the water ran out before the battle was over, the soldiers would have to survive on whatever they could capture—or die of thirst. Not a drop was wasted. Dirty water was hoarded and filtered for use in radiators.

Obtaining fresh water was crucial to survival. The standard water holder used by both sides was the $4\frac{1}{2}$-gallon container used by the Germans, and copied by the British, known as the Jerry can. Loaded with stacks of these receptacles, fleets of trucks crisscrossed the desert to bring water to in-

British Special Air Service raiders in patrol cars after a mission.

fantry outposts and tank brigades. Water could be distilled from the salty Mediterranean; after it was chemically treated, it was drinkable but unpleasant. When the British boiled the solution for tea and added canned milk, the milk curdled and sank to the bottom.

Lacking water, the soldiers scoured their uniforms with sand to cleanse them of oil and grime. When the British had gasoline to spare, they used it to wash clothes. Unless troops cleaned their shirts, shorts, and sweaters occasionally, their clothing became stiff with dirt and perspiration.

German ground troops wore field caps, light shirts, shorts, and high boots. Infantry on the line wore helmets. The general-issue uniform was made of green cotton. After long wear and frequent cleaning, however, the color faded to the shade of khaki worn by the British. When the Germans seized vast stocks of British uniforms at Tobruk, they issued the clothes to Axis units. As a consequence, except for DAK or Italian insignia, both sides wore almost the same uniform.

For amusement, Rommel's men wrote letters, played cards, bartered food, and traded with the Arabs for poultry and vegetables. For news they read the camp newspaper, *The Oasis*, or waited for the Luftwaffe to bring in mail from Germany. For a lucky few, there was leave to visit Benghazi where German and Italian movies were shown. Occasionally, fortunate soldiers had a rare bath in the sea. Some managed to share bottles of wine with their better-supplied Italian comrades.

But moments for relaxation were rare. Training was continuous, and patrolling ceaseless. Even when the front was quiet, there was always new equipment to master. Captured vehicles had to be repaired and overhauled regularly. By the process of "cannibalization," some totally disabled German and British tanks were refitted for use. To the men of the DAK Berlin seemed far away. Nazi propaganda about the triumph of Hitler's Third Reich meant little. The desert— with its dead, its barbed wire and shell craters, its cemeteries of burned vehicles—was their real world.

Although they were locked in savage combat, a strange bond developed between the opposing forces. This sense of identity occurred because the troops were isolated from Europe, and because they shared common dangers and discomforts. The desert opponents managed to maintain a respect for captives that was rare between Axis and Allied soldiers in World War II. Prisoners were treated with humanity and were provided the same food as their guards. Once a British officer complained to Rommel that his fellow prisoners were not receiving sufficient water. Standing in the blistering heat and longing for a cold drink to quench his own thirst, Rommel replied, "You are getting exactly the same ration as the Afrika Korps and myself—half a cup [daily]." When members of the Jewish Brigade were imprisoned after the DAK stormed Bir Hacheim, Rommel saw that they received the same treatment as other prisoners.

Flags of truce were respected, and firing automatically

ceased when medical teams displaying the Red Cross evacuated the wounded from the battlefield. German, Italian, British, French, American, and Commonwealth medical doctors all worked to ease the misery of their own wounded and those of the enemy. Medical tents full of men silent with pain, stunned from shell shock or loss of blood, or screaming in agony contained soldiers from both sides, all waiting for treatment. The most serious cases, whether friend or enemy, received priority. Those casualties who had a fair chance to survive a few more hours came next. Men with minor wounds were handled last. Doctors quickly decided which patients needed emergency surgery: the New Zealander with the concussion, the Italian with his chest shattered by bullets, or the German whose limb required amputation.

This comradeship of the desert was due to climatic conditions, similar hardships, and respect for traditional rules of war, and it was reinforced by a shared collection of stories. Originally true, the tales became legends in the retelling. There were dozens of jokes about the habits of British generals—particularly General Bernard Montgomery. There were ample laughs about the incompetence of some Italian divisions. One story, retold endless times around campfires, concerned a crafty German sergeant during the confusion of Operation Crusader. He put on the cap of a British military policeman, stood by a road, and calmly directed an Eighth Army convoy right into an Axis prison camp. There was the account of a British major, who was twice captured during a battle, and who twice escaped. Finally he reached safety by hiding in a well while a furious tank battle raged around him for hours.

Of course, there were plenty of stories about Rommel. The field marshal, a German paratrooper related, "had the strength of a horse. I never saw a man like him. No need for food, no need for drink, no need for sleep. He could wear out men twenty and thirty years younger." The "Africans" retold how Rommel was often seen pushing and hauling with his driver and aides to retrieve his car from soft sand. The field marshal was also famous for an incident at Tobruk where he joined his sappers in carefully probing in the sand with his hands for lethal mines. Another story related by the Australians was also true. During his first campaign in Cyrenaica, a young German lieutenant complained to Rommel that his tank was nearly out of gas. "Take your tank and capture some from the English" was Rommel's crisp reply.

One of the most popular stories told in the ranks of the Eighth demonstrated that Rommel was "a decent chap." During the fight for Sidi Rezegh, lines shifted frequently, and commanders were uncertain of unit locations, including medical facilities. A British medical team in an Eighth Army sector was treating wounded in tents. Out of a swirling sandstorm Rommel and some officers appeared. In the confusion, the British did not recognize the field marshal. Rommel approached Dr. Ian Aird, the chief physician, and asked to see General Fritz Stephan, a close German friend, whose chest and right lung had been ripped by shrapnel. Stephan had just received a blood transfusion, and surgery was under way. Assuming that the Desert Fox was a Polish ally, the doctor escorted Rommel through the tents. Some startled German wounded who recognized their commander tried to sit at attention. After watching the operation a few minutes, Rommel sensed that he would soon be detected. He thanked the medics for their treatment of his men, quickly left the hospital area, and drove off to rejoin the raging battle.

The link that united the Afrika Korps and the Eighth Army resulted from something more than common hardships and shared stories, however. It stemmed from the romantic voice of a woman they would never see. Every night at 2200, radios all over the desert were tuned to broadcasts from Rome. The troops listened to a sentimental ballad called "Lili Marlene," a sad, haunting song about a girl who waits for her soldier under a streetlight near a barracks gate. The tune reminded the troops of the girl back home. Sung in chorus around campfires, whistled in tents, or quietly hummed while on night duty, "Lili Marlene" became the unofficial anthem of the desert fighters.

In the desert, the tank was the major weapon, and the tank men—bronzed by the sun and caked with dust—were the chosen warriors. The riflemen and other nonmotorized troops had the grueling task of fighting in the open, exposed to the enemy, digging when the ground was hard to shovel, thirsty when water was scarce, trudging to the fight miles away, and trudging wearily back again. But armored crews had the advantage and confidence that came from traveling inside twenty-five tons of steel and plate, protected by a cannon and two machine guns. Tank men could drive across the barren wilderness as long as their fuel lasted.

At the cry, "Mount up," five black-uniformed men of a Panzer crew climbed through the round hatch on top of the thick steel turret and squirmed into their places. The driver, radio operator, and tank commander were unable to see each other, but they communicated by radio. The gunner and his loader sat closer together, but they too conversed by intercom. Inside, with the turret closed the heat became almost unbearable.

The Panzer tank was a small, roving fortress, powered by a 320-horsepower Mayback engine. Although a diesel engine would have been more suitable for Africa, the Italians—who had been experimenting with diesels for tanks—neglected to advise the Germans about their findings. Without experience in the Western Desert, the Germans had neglected to protect the engines from sand and dust. Consequently, in 1941 the life of a German engine was about fifteen hundred miles. By the spring of 1942, when special fittings were added, the duration of a tank engine was doubled, matching that of British armor.

The tanks surged over the battlefield, churning up dense clouds of sand. The noise inside was deafening during combat as the hot shell cases clattered on the deck. The gears cranked as the driver shifted up and down, then right or left. When the enemy was sighted, the tank stopped, the guns pounded until the enemy was destroyed or out of sight. Tank commanders feared the sight of enemy armor appearing on their flanks. They tried to move behind low rises, keeping their silhouettes hull-down to expose little of the machine's bulk.

Panzer crews performed very dangerous work. If their tank was immobilized by a fuel shortage, soft sand, or a mine, the lives of the crewmen were immediately endangered. An error in navigation, a failure in radio communication, a depletion of ammunition, or a jammed gun breach could mean being trapped in a raging inferno. The men worked in a mechanical bomb that contained 350 gallons of gasoline, 100 shells, and 3,700 machine gun bullets, all of which could explode and engulf them in flame if an enemy projectile exploded inside. If the hatch jammed, the crew could be roasted alive.

When a tank blew up, long tongues of flame would flicker out of every opening. The shells and bullets inside the blackened hulk exploded until the entire hull quivered and twisted in the death agony of a metal monster. Blistering streams of molten aluminum spouted out to congeal on the sand. Then the oil and rubber caught fire, and a spiral of black smoke rose from the blazing wreck. Crews who crawled outside their tanks toppled to the ground, writhing in pain as they tried to smother the flames on their bodies. There was nothing glamorous about such horror. The sight of blackened corpses and burned skeletons made the bravest men wonder about their own fate.

Tank men were up at 0500 to drive out on patrol, to guard an outpost, or to battle the enemy. Fights between armored forces usually occurred in the early morning or late afternoon on a north–south line. During combat, one army usually faced a blinding sun. Hence, the British preferred the morning with the sun at their back; the late afternoon gave the Axis troops an advantage. The haze of heat at noon was usually too great for fighting. The sun's rays on the sand caused severe eyestrain, frequent mirages, and shimmering heat waves. Vision was only slightly obscured from sunrise to 0900 and from

1500 to sundown. At those times, accurate vision varied between 2,000 and 5,000 yards. As the temperature rose during the day, the effective range of observation was limited to 1,500 yards.

Being a tank man was an exhausting and nerve-wracking way of life, particularly for tank commanders who tried to retain all-round vision before combat by standing erect. They had to keep their heads above the open turret and peer through the haze on all sides. Fumes, the noise of the clanking machinery, the need to wear headphones, and the lack of ventilation within the tank added to the strain and fatigue of the crew.

Panzer crews lusted for battle, for they were confident of their abilities. But they were greatly relieved when the day's fighting was over. Then they could open the hatch, hoist themselves out of the stifling oven, and enjoy the relative cool. The men would stretch out in the shadow of their Mark III, brew coffee on a small stove, eat some beans and biscuits, and relate the day's events. The rest of their time was spent refueling, replenishing ammunition, and repairing or maintaining their vehicle. Such tasks were usually finished by 2400. Each man did an hour's guard duty. Thus crews averaged about three hours of sleep each night. A week on the line was the usual limit of efficiency for most British tank men, but Rommel often kept his Panzers in action for two weeks at a time. Rommel's tank crews—like submarine and bomber crews—were a special breed of men who were frequently exposed to perils. They learned to tolerate the boredom, drudgery, and discomfort of the desert. Their comradeship was strengthened by sharing the same dangers, handling enormous mechanical power, and learning to outgun and outwit the enemy.

The nature of Afrika Korps was influenced by its rapid adjustment to the environment, by Rommel's personality, and by the military capabilities of the enemy. Other elements affecting the DAK were beyond its control: the army's distance from Europe, the attitude of the high command, and the cracking of the German code by the Allies.

Distance had the most obvious impact on the "Africans." There were no cities to loot in Libya, no cultivated lands to plunder. The ability of the desert to supply fuel, food, and materials was zero. Virtually everything that the DAK required had to be imported across the Mediterranean to Tripoli, whose manufacturing facilities never matched those in Cairo. All seaborne cargo came from four Italian ports to Tripoli, where only five ships could be unloaded at a time. Vessels waiting outside this major bottleneck were easy targets for the RAF. Neither Benghazi nor Tobruk had adequate docking arrangements, and only a trickle of supplies came through these harbors. About 85 percent of Axis supplies, 91 percent of personnel, and 92 percent of ships sent to Libya reached their destinations safely. But at critical moments in the campaigns, significant gaps and shortages occurred in Rommel's supply line. Requiring 70,000 tons of supplies monthly at El Alamein, the DAK could be doomed unless the logistical problems were solved.

In addition, the Afrika Korps had to rely on one coastal road from Tripoli that was constantly strafed by the RAF. In contrast, the Eighth had access to a railroad running from Alexandria to El Alamein. Further, the DAK was always handicapped by a shortage of trucks. Because Rommel overlooked the realities of the supply situation, the logistical strength of the Germans deteriorated in direct proportion to the distance they advanced into Egypt.

A second factor was the attitude of the German high command. Commanders need the support and confidence of the political leader at home and his military advisers. If a field marshal was distrusted in Berlin, his battle plans were changed, reinforcements were delayed, and threats and warnings came from his superiors at home. It was true that Hitler had selected Rommel for a vital role and that Nazi propaganda popularized the Desert Fox. But the führer's plans for North Africa constantly wavered and shifted. Thus the DAK was often prevented from performing to its ability because Hitler incorrectly judged the situation. And every time he ignored Hitler's orders, Rommel gambled with his life. The Nazis executed German generals who disobeyed Hitler.

Unfortunately for Rommel, because of his middle-class background and his occasional insubordination, no one in the high command pleaded his case. Rommel was a self-made field marshal who barely concealed his contempt for his superiors at home. Furthermore, in comparison with the mighty struggle being waged on the Russian front, the North African theater seemed to Hitler's advisers like a senseless expenditure of men and material. Even a possible victory over the British was considered not strategically significant compared with a defeat of the Russians at Stalingrad. Thus, because of the indifference in Berlin, the Afrika Korps never received the support it needed.

The last factor was completely unknown to Rommel, but it was of great importance throughout the campaigns. This was the contribution of "Ultra" to Allied victory. Ultra was the name given in 1938 by the British to top-secret information decoded from the German intelligence device—the "Enigma" machine. Enigma was a complex electronic mechanism on which the Germans encoded messages and signals transmitted by radio between the high command and its operational centers all over Europe. By 1939 the British had learned to intercept and decode these signals, providing London with vital information about German activities on all fronts: bomber flights, ship convoys, troop deployments, location of U-boats, and so forth. Throughout the war, the Germans were completely unaware that their code had been cracked because of the tight security that the British kept on Ultra. The Germans were supremely confident that their complicated scrambling of signals could not possibly be understood by the enemy.

Soon after the Afrika Korps arrived in Libya, in February

1941, a branch of Ultra was established in Cairo. Thereafter, Rommel's opponents received transcripts of the signals sent between Tripoli, Rome, and Berlin. The interception and decoding by Ultra of the radio transmissions about ship convoys in the Mediterranean were of enormous value to the RAF and the Royal Navy in striking at Axis shipping with accuracy. Knowledge about Rommel's supplies, reinforcements, and battle plans were obviously useful to Wavell and Auchinleck. But because of misinterpretation of data, delays in decoding, and incompetence of British intelligence in Egypt, the vital information was not a major factor in British strategy until the summer of 1942. Likewise, Ultra information was so precious that it was restricted to the British commander in chief in Cairo and a few of his subordinates. Thus, the need for security limited the amount of secret information about the DAK that filtered down to divisional commanders. Even so, it is clear that Rommel's command was handicapped from the start. Nevertheless, the Afrika Korps demonstrated an amazing degree of energy against enormous odds as it prepared to continue the fight in the Western Desert.

9
THE CAULDRON

AFTER THE British victory in Crusader, logistics tended to favor Rommel. As the Eighth Army marched westward, it was subject to the relentless law of supply on the desert. The Afrika Korps was only five hundred miles from its main base at Tripoli, while the Eighth's routes stretched a thousand miles back to Egypt. By January 17 Rommel was aware that Ritchie was overextended and that he had been ordered to withdraw veteran units for service in the Far East. Now the Fox planned a surprise counterattack. Informing only his top staff of his aims, Rommel shifted his forces forward during darkness, ordering the burning of ships and buildings along the coast to suggest another retreat. Keeping his plan a secret even from the high command, Rommel began his offensive at night on January 21, 1942, by coincidence a night of heavy rain, followed by blinding sandstorms.

His attack caught the enemy by surprise. In furnacelike heat, Rommel led Ariete, Trieste, and German motorized groups along the Via Balbia. To the south, parallel with the highway, Crüwell directed the Panzers. Rommel's wing drove north, scattered British outposts, and captured Antelat on January 22. Soon afterward, Ariete seized the town of Saunnu to the east. Rommel pressed his luck. He scattered the unprepared Eighth Army and easily seized Agedabia and Beda Fomm. Throwing caution to the winds as his raid developed into an offensive, Rommel continued to probe eastward. He sensed that his enemy was baffled about where to defend.

Ignoring orders from Rome that he pause to consolidate, Rommel drove on. By January 30 the Panzers had shattered the newly arrived Second Armored Brigade. Here was an example of another basic difference between the German and the British armies. The British reinforced unit by unit, pulling complete brigades and divisions out of the line, replacing them with fresh organizations composed of raw troops. The Germans retained their divisions on the front and reinforced them with fresh troops in small numbers. Thus, a unit's pride and know-how were preserved and transmitted to the newcomers. Rarely was an untried German regiment thrown hastily into battle. Likewise, the Afrika Korps never fought with untested tanks. As a result, it had a core of battle-tested veterans and dependable equipment for every conflict, while the British exposed fresh troops and unreliable armor.

The next phase of the campaign was dramatic. On January 27 Rommel thrust eastward at Msus and Mechili, just as the British assumed he would. But he quickly shifted his forces north and then west to Benghazi, throwing the surprised British command off guard. On January 29 the Fourth Indian Division, unable to shield Benghazi without armor, prepared to retire. In a comedy of tragic errors, Ritchie, and then Auchinleck, reversed the retreat order on the assumption that Rommel's tanks were out of fuel.

In Parliament on January 26, Churchill lumbered to his feet in order to counter criticism by the political opposition over the latest crisis in Africa. The Eighth Army was losing in Cyrenaica, he admitted, and again newspapers were proclaiming the exploits of the Desert Fox. In a tribute unique to a German enemy, Churchill stated: "We have a very daring and skillful opponent against us, and, may I say, across the havoc of war, a great general." Soon after his speech, an Axis motorized column burst from the escarpment in drenching rain, deployed across the Via Balbia, and trapped the entire

Indian division. Benghazi and Derna, to the east, had tons of gasoline and 13,000 vehicles to sustain the momentum of the DAK. In Derna, a departing British soldier chalked on a wall a reminder of the seesaw contest for North Africa: "Please keep tidy. Be back soon." Again outwitted, the Eighth fell back to the familiar Gazala Line on February 6. In the recovery of the Cyrenaican bulge, the DAK again demonstrated its professionalism. It fused rapidly at critical moments. It avoided tactical errors, and, as usual, Rommel provided dynamic leadership. Until the spring, the Afrika Korps rested. Now an uneasy lull typified the campaign as the opposing sides at Gazala watched each other.

Hitler was overjoyed at the DAK's victories. He awarded the fifty-one-year-old Rommel more military decorations and promoted him to the rank of colonel general, the youngest in the Wehrmacht. The führer also raised the Afrika Korps from a mere corps to a full army (*Panzergruppe*). Henceforth, Rommel was a commander in chief with more authority, particularly in dealing with the sometimes quarrelsome Italian officers. More troops flowed in. Two fresh Italian divisions arrived, along with the tough First Paratroop Brigade under General Hermann Ramcke from Crete. Experts in tank warfare joined Rommel's staff. Walther Nehring became chief of staff; Georg von Bismarck became commander of the Twenty-first Panzers, and Gustav von Vaerst took over the Fifteenth Panzers. In two whirlwind weeks, Rommel had driven the enemy back 250 miles, recovered his reputation, and raised the morale of his troops.

Basking in the glory, Rommel let his triumphs fire his imagination. Could he crack the heavily mined Gazala Line? Could the DAK capture Tobruk and then invade Egypt? If so, Rommel knew that his soldiers would follow him to Cairo, the Nile, the Red Sea, and even Iraq. As Baron Hans-Karl von Esebeck, a German staff correspondent, explained: "There is this strange magnetic strength that this soldier radiates to his troops, right down to the last rifleman. . . . When [Rommel] talks to them he calls a spade a spade; he uses hard language with them, but he also knows how to praise and encourage them"

Malta, with its British air base, was temporarily neutralized in the spring by German pilots, and Rommel received men and equipment at an unprecedented rate. Malta was the strategic key in the Mediterranean. In March, Hitler and Mussolini ordered that the island be captured in early June by air and sea assaults—a plan known as Operation Hercules. But Rommel used his personal influence with the high command to have Hercules delayed three weeks. On April 30 he received permission from Berlin and from Rome to attack the Gazala Line, capture Tobruk, and then turn on the defensive to wait for events in the Mediterranean. With Tobruk captured, Malta would be the next Axis objective. Smothering that tiny island and besieging Tobruk could not occur simultaneously. So Tobruk came first.

As future operations would reveal, the Axis partners made a crucial error in timing for Malta. That island, not Tobruk, should have had the higher priority in their battle plans. In May 1942, with a strong Luftwaffe and ample airborne troops, opposed by only a feeble RAF and Royal Navy, it would have been possible for the Axis to capture Malta. The potential benefits of the island as a base for German planes and submarines were immeasurable. But, by late May, when Rommel hit the Gazala Line, the Axis had committed itself to battle in the desert, not at sea.

The importance of Malta impressed Churchill. He and his military advisers in London ordered Auchinleck to attack the DAK in order to secure airfields in Cyrenaica that could aid the RAF in protecting convoys. Just as Auchinleck was preparing to attack, Rommel launched an offensive at the Gazala Line on May 26.

The months of peace, reinforcements, and training were reflected in the DAK's strength. German tank losses from Operation Crusader were remedied by reinforcements of over two hundred Mark IIIs with thicker armor and improved guns. Rommel also received eighteen Mark IVs with an improved 75-millimeter high-velocity shell. Altogether, Rommel had four hundred German tanks and over two hundred Italian tanks. He had forty-eight 88s, twenty Czech 75-millimeter guns, about eighty 50-millimeter guns, and some Russian anti-tank guns. The army was rested, and prospects for victory seemed high.

But as in the past, the British had the advantage of strength. Ritchie faced Rommel with over eight hundred tanks, and more were on the way. His surprise for the enemy was the new Grant; he had seventy-five of them. The American tank had extremely thick armor, weighed 28 tons, and had a 75-millimeter gun, at last providing the British with a tank that would fire a high-explosive shell from a long range at the 88s. But few suspected that the Grant's low-hung gun with its small traverse was a grave weakness. Furthermore, it was a tall machine, and it had to be exposed on the horizon in order to fire its salvo, in contrast to the hull-down position favored by the Panzers. Still, it was new to the DAK, and it could upset Rommel's timetable.

Not only did Ritchie outnumber Rommel roughly two to one in tanks, but he also had a three-to-two advantage in artillery and a seven-to-five advantage in planes. Against Rommel's 113,000 troops, Ritchie commanded 125,000. With two armored divisions, the First and Seventh, along with various tank brigades, two South African divisions, the British Fiftieth Division, the Free French, and several mobile brigades, Ritchie possessed a formidable force. Likewise, his defense at Gazala was strong. The line stretched forty-five miles from the coast to its anchor in the desert at Bir Hacheim. The Gazala front was protected by 500,000 mines placed for two to three miles over the desert tracks. Behind these mine fields were six "boxes," about a mile square, manned by brigades ready to smash Axis penetrations.

Rommel took a chance. Leaving some Italian tanks in the

north to cover his defense, he decided to mount a broad sweep of his armor to the south. The attack came on May 26. As an opening distraction, Crüwell led two Italian infantry corps and one brigade to the northern Gazala Line. Rommel intended Crüwell to feint here to divert some British armor from the center and the south. Crüwell's assault began at 0200. At 0430 Rommel's Panzers and Ariete thundered south. Within two days, Rommel confidently predicted, Tobruk would be his.

While Crüwell's troops battled near the coast, Rommel led 10,000 vehicles south and then east in a great sweep past Bir Hacheim. Everything had been carefully calculated—speeds, distances, compass bearings, and rations for seven days. Flickering flames concealed in empty gasoline cans guided the columns, and the Luftwaffe dropped flares to illuminate difficult terrain. With the smoothness of a well-oiled machine, the Afrika Korps moved over the desert. Every unit was in formation. Armored cars led the procession. The tanks came next, followed by the artillery, mobile infantry, and antitank guns. In the center of the divisional formations were the "thin-skinned" supply vehicles. By 0300 on May 27 Rommel's advanced units were at Bir Hacheim, forty miles south of Tobruk. There the Panzers rested and refueled.

But in spite of the smooth maneuver, near chaos resulted. Rommel's armor was spotted at dawn by an observation post near Bir Hacheim. "Looks like a brigade of Jerry tanks coming. It's more than a brigade," reported an excited British scout to headquarters. "It's the whole bloody Afrika Korps." The British were not duped by Crüwell's thrust at the northern end of the line, and thus the British deployed more armor to the south. Ariete was unable to budge the defiant French at Bir Hacheim. Even the Ninetieth Light reached El Adem three hours late. The British kept their armored brigades closer together than Rommel had anticipated, and resistance in the south increased hour by hour.

Rommel's advance was stalling. With his bold end run, he

had again overextended the DAK. The Ninetieth was stranded at El Adem, Fifteenth Panzer was nearly out of fuel, and Ariete was immobile at Bir Hacheim. Although the DAK eliminated enemy brigades that crossed its route that afternoon, it suffered heavy losses. By evening, one-third of the Panzers were disabled or burning hulks.

Not only had Ritchie been prepared for Rommel's offensive, but the Eighth had a new tank and a new artillery piece. Panzer commanders stared through their binoculars at the unfamiliar silhouette of the giant Grant tank with its main gun in the side turret. The Grant was about equal in fire power to the Mark IV. It hurled explosive shells from a 75-millimeter gun in its hull and poured 37-millimeter ammunition on Axis ground troops from its revolving turret. The psychological impact of the Grant was awesome, as the Germans watched their 50-millimeter ammunition bounce off its sides. As Rommel remarked, "The advent of the new American tank had torn great holes in our ranks." Furthermore, at Gazala, the British demonstrated their six-pounder, a 57-millimeter antitank gun that had devastating penetrating power.

Rommel raced around the smoking battlefield seeking information, often standing upright in a vehicle to encourage his men. So confusing was the encounter in the dust and haze that low-flying Luftwaffe pilots were unable to determine which units were enemy and which were friendly. At one point a squadron of Stukas found a clearing in the sky and dive-bombed the British tanks. This air support provided Rommel with the opportunity to remove his armor from a losing encounter. His army was widely dispersed, his supplies sparse, and his own headquarters had been demolished by shellfire. But battle plans of generals often change, and Rommel was a master of improvisation during an emergency.

Aware that he was losing the contest, Rommel raced back around the tip of the Gazala Line to his base for supplies. On May 28 he returned with 1,500 vehicles laden with fuel and ammunition for his hard-pressed Panzers. But even this emergency blood transfusion was enough for only one more day of fighting. Luckily for the DAK, the Trieste Division on early May 29 managed to find a small footpath through the mine fields. This route to the west became Rommel's lifeline. Now he could avoid the long detour south for supplies and tap his depots due east beyond the mine fields.

By May 29 Rommel's wide sweep was over. It was now a question of survival. With his back to the mine fields, Rommel pulled back all his armor into a tight defensive semicircle on the Trigh Capuzzo. With his tanks kept hull down and his 88s providing a screen to halt British armored pressure from the east, Rommel hoped to hack a route through the deadly mine fields. Until his sappers removed the mines and cleared a road for supply trucks, the DAK was trapped in the "Cauldron," as it became known for its seething outbursts of volcanic fighting.

The major obstacle in the middle of Rommel's route went to safety was the Knightsbridge box. It contained the 150th Guards Brigade and the Fourth Royal Tank Brigade. Until this obstacle was overcome, Rommel was encircled. Thus, on May 30, the Afrika Korps had to hold in the east, eliminate the Knightsbridge box, clear a path through the mines, link up with the Italian infantry in the north, smash Bir Hacheim, and open up a desert flank. Could Rommel achieve these objectives? The DAK was being chewed up hour by hour and seemed about to disintegrate. Both Nehring and Bayerlein urged Rommel to surrender.

But Rommel's luck held. Ritchie's troops struck hard at the Cauldron from May 29 through May 31. But the British tanks were repulsed by the DAK's gun screen, and the armored brigades failed to coordinate their attacks. Only minor attempts were made to relieve the Knightsbridge box, which was surrounded by German troops. The British riflemen and tanks there were left unsupported in three days of fighting.

Rommel took advantage of Ritchie's slow reaction. He had the Luftwaffe strafe the troublesome stronghold, and Rommel himself scrambled with his infantry to direct ground assaults. The Twenty-first Panzers to the north of the box and the Fifteenth Panzers to the south shattered the last resistance. At dusk on June 1 the DAK finally captured the three thousand British troops at Knightsbridge who had nearly turned the tide of battle. Now the route to the west was enlarged, and supply trucks poured through to replenish Rommel's command.

Ritchie still failed to realize that Rommel was not retreating but regrouping. Not until June 5 did the Eighth Army launch several attacks on the Cauldron's rim. The assaults were described as sticking a hand into a wasps' nest. Rommel then counterattacked and overran the headquarters of two tank brigades and two infantry divisions, thus causing a paralysis of British communications. By now, two-thirds of Ritchie's tanks on the line were disabled. Many of his field and antitank guns were demolished, and four thousand of his troops were captured.

The turning point of the Cauldron battle was the huge loss of British armor on June 5 and 6. Rommel's tanks gradually approached parity with Ritchie's battered armored brigades. The clue to Rommel's success in this grueling fight is that the DAK fought continually; it regrouped, attacked again, and constantly maneuvered for position. It simultaneously held off heavy armored thrusts from the east, hit the 150th Guards Brigade box, carved out a supply route, and maintained the siege of Bir Hacheim.

Now with the enemy repulsed at the Cauldron, Rommel ordered an all-out attack on Bir Hacheim. At this stone fortress were 3,600 Free French and several hundred members of the Jewish Legion. The small garrison resisted heroically, but again the British failed to reinforce a crucial point. The defenders held out against artillery fire, infantry assaults, and tank fire. Rommel then called for Junker 88s, Stuka dive-bombers, and Messerschmitt 109Fs to pulverize the bastion. Even then, the Germans had to haul up heavy guns to demolish the fortress. Bir Hacheim finally toppled on June 11.

Rommel admitted that "Seldom in Africa was I given such a hard-fought struggle."

Still blundering, Ritchie meanwhile failed to withdraw the First South African Division and a brigade of the Fiftieth Division from the coastal northern sector of the Gazala Line. On June 11 Rommel launched several thrusts from the escarpment to trap the British infantry. Here, British armor fought to the death to protect its ground troops. The Seventh Armored Division made a valiant effort to hold off the Panzers. Yet Rommel concentrated his armor with the Ninetieth Light and proceeded to destroy the Seventh bit by bit. Another one hundred Stuarts and Crusaders were lost in this encounter on June 10. The Germans benefited from having Rommel with them. While he hurried from one unit to another, he was bombed, shelled, machine-gunned, and often pinned down under fire. But Rommel was always aware of developments on the front. In contrast, the commander of the Seventh Armored was nearly captured and had to hide in a water tank. Consequently, his command lacked overall control for hours.

With the fall of Bir Hacheim and the crunch on the northern Gazala Line, the Afrika Korps resumed the offensive. Rommel had only 150 German and 60 Italian tanks functioning. But they continued to pounce on isolated enemy armor. On June 12, for instance, they captured or disabled another 140 British tanks in separate engagements, leaving Ritchie with only 70 on the line. The British were unable to extricate their vehicles, and German mechanics repaired scores of damaged Stuarts and Crusaders for use by the DAK. By June 14 the entire Gazala Line had collapsed. El Adem, Acroma, and Belhamed had all toppled by June 18. By then, Ritchie possessed only half of Rommel's strength, and he had to retreat to Tobruk.

The men on both sides were nearing exhaustion. The lack of trained British tank crews at a crucial moment was particularly apparent at Tobruk. Auchinleck had planned to include Tobruk in a new defensive line. He sent Churchill a message of confidence that the Eighth would hold a new position there and that Tobruk would not be evacuated. But Auchinleck in Cairo was unaware of the speed at which the Eighth Army was disintegrating, and Ritchie was uncertain about whether to establish a defensive zone to cover Tobruk or withdraw the Eighth from the area, leaving Tobruk to face a siege.

While Ritchie's staff debated the matter, the Fifteenth Panzers drove along the Via Balbia to Tobruk. By June 15 the Twenty-first Panzer Division was back at Sidi Rezegh. After the British Fourth Armored Brigade lost another thirty-two of its ninety tanks to the Panzers, the ring began to close around the fortress. Soon after the RAF evacuated its airfield at Gambut, the Twenty-first Panzers seized the area, and the investment of Tobruk was complete.

Now the Afrika Korps had to work fast. The invasion of Malta was scheduled for June 21, following the capture of Tobruk. In terms of sheer physical capacity, and with deteriorating equipment, the DAK seemed unable to meet the timetable. The German troops were so weary they were unable to prevent the Second South African Division from slipping through to the fortress. But Rommel was determined to seize Tobruk quickly and ruthlessly. Now the great prize that had restricted his mobility and had curtailed his supplies was finally within his grasp, if his men moved swiftly. Ignoring the fact that his men were exhausted, he ordered an attack on the citadel for June 20.

The tide of war was now in Rommel's favor. Auchinleck lacked a plan to defend Tobruk. Ritchie assumed that the fortress could hold out for two months, but he ignored the brutal truth of Tobruk's vulnerability. Ritchie even neglected to provide Major General H. B. Klopper, the fortress commander, with specific orders for defending the post. Granted the city had three million rations of food, seven thousand tons of water, well over a million gallons of gasoline, and thousands of rounds of ammunition. But its garrison was unprepared for the attack. Klopper had assumed that Tobruk would be part of a large defensive system, that it would not be left to protect itself. Naturally the morale of his troops fell as thousands of Commonwealth soldiers hurried through the city to safety in the east.

Klopper commanded a miscellaneous assortment of men who had never functioned together. They had enough artillery, but it was widely scattered and its barrages were uncoordinated. Even the obstacles that had impeded the Germans in the past were less difficult. Thousands of mines and miles of barbed wire had been removed months before for use on the Gazala Line. Numerous pillboxes and strong points had deteriorated. Trenches and antitank ditches were now silted from a year's accumulation of drifting sand. Klopper was certainly not the defiant General Morshead, and the defenders of Tobruk were not the fierce Ninth Australian Division.

By contrast, Rommel had a sensible battle plan and an experienced team to carry it out. His men had been preparing for trench tactics for months, and they knew the terrain. By deceptive movements of troops around the perimeter, Rommel concealed his intentions as to where he would attack. At 0520 on June 20 he unleashed a massive artillery saturation at the weak southeast sector. Then he sent in 200 planes that Kesselring had dispatched from Crete, Greece, and Africa to smash the line. Guided by smoke bombs, the Luftwaffe provided close ground support. The RAF was nowhere in sight. After the front lines were obliterated by the pounding, German and Italian infantry darted through the choking dust and fumes. They overran trenches, assaulted strong points, and demolished bunkers. The riflemen were quickly followed by sappers, who removed mines, and by engineers, who erected steel bridges over the ditches. By 0830 that day the Panzers were rolling over the metal pathway through geysers of dust as they tore through the heart of the fortress. Rommel's plan went off like the clockwork of a master craftsman. Bunker after bunker, observation posts, and even Fort Solaro and Fort Pilastrino fell to the Axis troops. At 1400 the tanks crept up the escarpment, and finally their crews could peer down at the city and its harbor. After months of back-breaking toil, crouching in the sun under withering artillery fire, freezing at night, and being bitten day after day by insects, after months of heat and thirst, the DAK had finally stormed Tobruk. And this was the citadel that Churchill had compared to Gibraltar, saying it could never topple.

Oddly enough, the capture of Tobruk, one of Rommel's greatest victories, was not a tank battle, but a siege like the Battle of Verdun during World War I. The fortress that had held out for eight months fell in one day. At dawn on June 21 the white flag of surrender was hoisted by the beaten foe. Churchill was conferring in Washington with Franklin D. Roosevelt, the President of the United States, about future strategy when he received the tragic news. "This was one of the heaviest blows I can recall during the war," he remembered. "Defeat is one thing; disgrace is another."

In this stunning victory, the Afrika Korps captured 32,000 troops, 200 guns, 30 tanks, hundreds of vehicles, and huge quantities of supplies. Rommel's men shouted with delight at the stocks of food and clothing they discovered in the bulging warehouses. There were over 5,000 tons of provisions alone: pure white flour for bread, Irish potatoes, canned vegetables, preserves, cigarettes, gallons of whiskey, tins of canned meat, piles of khaki clothing, and boxes full of soft suede shoes with thick rubber soles. It seemed like a huge treasure chest. But the big prize for the thirsty soldiers was a cache of cases crammed with familiar brown, stubby bottles of Bavaria's famous Löwenbräu beer, imported from Lisbon.

Rommel dispatched a report of his triumph to Berlin. Then he quietly celebrated his victory by dining on a can of pineapple from South Africa, courtesy of the British quartermaster. Later, he courteously received a group of captured officers. Rommel smiled at them and then remarked: "Gentlemen, for you the war is over. You have fought like lions and have been led by donkeys."

10
THE ROAD TO CAIRO

ON JANUARY 21 German pilots reported that the Eighth Army was in full retreat to the Egyptian border. Rommel called on his troops to press on to the frontier—to Alexandria, to fabled Cairo, and to the glittering Nile. "Now for the complete destruction of the enemy," Rommel proclaimed. "During the days to come, I shall call on you for one more great effort to bring us to our final goal."

Hitler was overjoyed with the victory. German armies under Paulus in Russia were approaching Stalingrad. Another army under General Ewald von Kleist was invading the Russian Caucasus. Rommel was afire with dreams of conquest. If he had the resources that had been diverted from the attack on Malta, he claimed, he could drive on to the Nile. Thus, with Hitler's approval, the assault on Malta was postponed until September when Rommel would march through Cairo. The führer made Rommel a field marshal, again the youngest in the German army. Proud of his exploits and his new rank, Rommel nevertheless confided to his wife that he would have preferred not the promotion but another Panzer division.

The Panzers and the Ariete Division snapped at the heels of the Eighth Army as it scurried into Egypt. Bardia fell to the Germans. Sidi Barrani was captured. On June 23 Rommel's army crossed the border, hurrying to catch the enemy before it could establish a defense line. Typical of the field marshal's fondness for bluffing, he had the enemy on the run with only 60 Panzer tanks and 8,500 infantrymen fit for combat. Most of his vehicles were captured ones, and his officers played a new game with them. Dressed in khakis like the Eighth Army soldiers, and driving trucks with British markings, the Germans casually pulled alongside British infantry units on the march, waved at them, and then calmly rounded them up as prisoners. It was dangerous, but for Rommel's men, an exciting sport.

Yet a key factor in the drive into Egypt was the diminishing ability of the Afrika Korps to maintain the frenzied pace of recent weeks. The men seemed to be passing the peak of their strength. After weeks of driving and fighting with little sleep, soldiers began to doze in their vehicles. Hundreds of riflemen fell to the sides of the Trigh Capuzzo to sleep in the sand, oblivious to the scorching sun. The Twenty-first Panzer Division had innumerable breakdowns and could not maintain the momentum that Rommel decreed. And as the DAK approached Mersa Matruh, 120 miles inside Egypt, there were signs that the Eighth was regrouping. The Afrika Korps captured fewer prisoners. German radio interceptions picked up reports of a steady flow of tank brigades and infantry divisions into the Nile Delta. Malta, reinforced by Allied convoys, sent waves of bombers to hit Rommel's coastal traffic. The RAF intensified its strafing. Rommel had to hurl himself to the floor of his Mammoth as a Hurricane zoomed in at zero altitude to riddle his command car with shells.

It took time for the Eighth Army to reorganize. Most of its armor was either worn out or being repaired. The artillery was still disorganized. The infantry was demoralized, and it would find no safe lodgement from the dreaded Panzers until it reached a rail station named El Alamein (or Alamein), sixty miles beyond Mersa Matruh. But the major problem was in the command. Auchinleck removed Ritchie on June 25 and assumed charge of the Eighth in the field himself. His confusing directives made divisional commanders too cautious about their defense at poorly mined Mersa Matruh. They would have preferred to stand and fight another day with terrain to their advantage. Thus the Eighth was unprepared materially and psychologically when the DAK attacked on June 26.

Auchinleck had 185 tanks at Mersa Matruh. The town was held by the Tenth Indian Division. On the nearby escarpment was the Fiftieth Division. Due south was the First New Zealand Division, and farther west were two brigades of armor. The RAF held the sky.

Rommel had sixty Panzers and forty Italian tanks. He was short on infantry. He had supplies for only ten days, for his lines now reached a thousand miles to Tripoli. No Luftwaffe planes were available to assist. Auchinleck had called Rommel's bluff and was determined to hold.

But what happened instead was a series of blunders by the Eighth. Risking his depleted Ninetieth Division to threaten Mersa Matruh, Rommel merged all his armor to hit the British tanks to the south. Rommel's attack was so dispersed and so poorly coordinated that he should have lost the battle.

Yet British intelligence was as faulty as the Germans'. It credited the DAK with four times its actual tank strength. The British First Armored Division pulled back and left the New Zealanders alone to fight their way out. By June 27 Mersa Matruh was in Rommel's hands as the Eighth continued to retreat another sixty miles to El Alamein. The legend of the Desert Fox and the professionalism of the Afrika Korps were in full bloom. The bitter moment of truth had arrived. Either Auchinleck would stand and fight at El Alamein, or he would concede all of Egypt to Rommel.

As a result of their defeat at Mersa Matruh, the British prepared to demolish water lines, supply stations, ammunition depots, and power stations all the way to Cairo, where a state of emergency was declared. The Royal Navy prepared to evacuate Alexandria, a unique case of battleships being driven to sea by tanks. Still reeling over the loss of Tobruk, Churchill was battling for his political life during heated Parliamentary debates. In a blast of brilliant oratory, Churchill warded off a motion of censure of his government over the conduct of the war. Stories about Rommel and the supposed invincibility of the DAK swamped the bars and clubs in Cairo. In Alexandria a major bank paid out huge sums to depositors who panicked at the impending German occupation of Egypt. Even Auchinleck's headquarters in Cairo burned records and secret documents. So noticeable were the ashes and smoke over the city from such fires on July 1 that the day became known as "Ash Wednesday." The Egyptian press added to the fears. It announced that Mussolini had flown to Tripoli with a specially designed uniform for his triumphant entry into Cairo. According to the press, a white stallion, his mount for the symbolic restoration of the Roman Empire in the Middle East, had arrived on a transport plane in Benghazi.

Yet beneath these demonstrations of fear, the Eighth Army slowly began to recover. Any observer would have seen that the troops were tired and humiliated from successive defeats. But at El Alamein, 240 miles inside Egypt and 60 miles from Cairo, Auchinleck had a unique defense position. From the sea north of El Alamein stretched the British line 45 miles south to the Qattara Depression, the last natural defense before Cairo. Stretching 60 miles from east to west, the Qattara Depression is a huge saucerlike basin in the earth's surface about 200 to 600 feet below sea level. It is marked by a lack of sand dunes, wide cracks in the ground, deep winding wadis, and a morass of impenetrable white salt marshes. No vehicles had ever crossed it. The depression is so desolate that even camel caravans avoid it, and Arabs believe the area is haunted by ghosts.

The line at Alamein thus was unique, for it was virtually the only place in North Africa that had two protective flanks—the sea and the depression. As a result, Rommel would be unable to attempt his favorite wide-flanking maneuvers and would have to hit the Eighth with a frontal assault. Fascinated by this geological oddity that inhibited his movement, Rommel spent hours on the rim of the depression, wondering if his tanks could cross it.

Safe on the north and the south, Auchinleck began to construct a forty-five-mile line with three main boxes about fifteen
miles apart, supported by numerous small boxes. A key feature
of his defense was Ruweisat Ridge, which ran almost due east
and west, and which bisected the line. To the north, Auchinleck placed the Thirtieth Corps; to the south, the Thirteenth
Corps. Weak in infantry and artillery, and with only fifty-five
tanks in operation, Auchinleck hoped for reinforcements before Rommel struck.

Unwilling to give the enemy a chance to strengthen the El
Alamein Line, and believing that he had as much armor as
Auchinleck had, Rommel tried a quick thrust on July 1. Many
mistakes marred Rommel's first sortie at El Alamein. The Panzers became entangled on the night of June 30 and were several hours behind schedule. Hit by a blinding sandstorm, the
Ninetieth Light ran right into the El Alamein box and was
devastated by artillery fire. The Ninetieth was so badly mauled
that it panicked, a rarity for the DAK. Because of its late
start, the Afrika Korps advanced into the morning sun and was
repulsed by concentrated artillery fire.

And worse would follow. As the Panzers swung south they
discovered an unsuspected sector west of Ruweisat Ridge. In
a well-defended depression, the Eighth Indian Brigade stopped
the German tanks in their tracks with accurate fire from their
twenty-three field guns and sixteen 6-pounder antitank guns,
thereby providing time for British armor to regroup and attack.
By evening, the DAK had only thirty-seven tanks, and the
Suez Canal looked far away. The irony of the situation is that
the British were again too cautious and failed to appreciate
how badly Rommel's units had been battered.

The field marshal tried again on July 2 and 3 near the coast,
but he was uncertain of the box locations. His ground troops
were mauled, and he lost another eleven tanks to concealed
guns. The British were finally mastering the German technique
of hiding their gun screens and were retaliating for past losses
with lethal revenge. Everywhere that Rommel probed for an
opening—in the north, center, or south—he encountered bit-

ter resistance. And the RAF lashed back at his armor with savage fury. Even the plucky Arietes' morale sagged on July 3 when New Zealanders crashed through Italian outposts in one sector and captured their field guns. On July 4 Rommel ended his thrusts and allowed his men to rest. He admitted that the resistance was too great. He had already lost four thousand men at El Alamein without denting Auchinleck's line.

Auchinleck called the tune for the next few weeks. Fighting occurred all over the line, some of which was good tank terrain but other parts of which were full of soft powdery sand. Dominating the area was blood-soaked Ruweisat Ridge. Here the DAK fought to a standstill, and here the Eighth made a fresh start.

Auchinleck began his thrusts on July 7 with an attempt to ram the Eighth's armor around Rommel's desert flank. On the night of July 9, Rommel was awakened by the loudest noise he had heard since World War I. Auchinleck had fooled the Fox. He had unleashed a massive artillery barrage in the far north. This attack was the clue to Auchinleck's strategy in July: to force Rommel's armor into one sector and then destroy his Italian allies in another by relentlessly grinding them down division by division. In the attack on Tell el Eisa, the Australians overran Rommel's headquarters, captured his entire command staff, and returned with Rommel's battle plans, field reports, and code book. Mellenthin barely managed to hold here by rushing in fresh German troops newly arrived from Crete.

On July 12 the Eighth's target was the Trieste Division, another weak link in Rommel's line. Again Rommel had to rush in his Panzers and German infantry to save his Italian allies. But the Sabratha Division was knocked out on July 9, the Brescia Division on July 15, Trento and Trieste on July 17, and the Ariete Armored Division was barely functioning by July 30.

Though Auchinleck had found the formula to keep the

DAK off balance, the Eighth Army was still not ready for a decisive breakthrough. The Eighth's weakness was its armor. This was clear on July 14 when Auchinleck attempted to capture all of Ruweisat Ridge. The Eighth held the eastern side of the 700-foot slope, and the Italians held the western side. Auchinleck aimed to clear the Pavia and Brescia divisions from the ridge. Under the attack, Brescia collapsed, and by dawn the Commonwealth infantry was on the verge of capturing the entire ridge. But where was the British Twenty-second Armored, which was supposed to support the infantry? By error, it never appeared. Rommel quickly sent in Panzers, engulfed the entire New Zealand brigade, and recovered the western slope by July 16. Life had been needlessly wasted. Clearly, the Eighth was at fault in training and leadership. Ruweisat was the bitter fruit of this carelessness.

The determined Auchinleck tried another approach on July 21, hitting not at the Italians, but at the DAK. By now, Rommel had lost half his artillery and half his antitank guns. He had 42 German tanks and 50 Italian tanks functioning. The prospects of victory for the Eighth seemed good. Auchinleck had 173 cruiser tanks in the First Armored Division and 150 infantry tanks in the Twenty-third Armored Division. The plan was to attack at night west and south of the ridge. The infantry assaults went smoothly. But the Panzers, ready at dawn on the slopes, proceeded to destroy the unprotected British troops. The men of the Twenty-third Armored appeared too late and from the wrong direction. They advanced right into the line of German mines, guns, and tanks. Over 87 Valentine and Matilda tanks were destroyed or disabled in one of the worst disasters to British armor in a single action. In the fight, nineteen-year-old Corporal Gunther Helm, manning his 88 with cool precision, demolished four Valentines in two minutes. Then he quickly shot four more tanks to pieces before his station was wrecked by gunfire. For his exploits, Helm became the first enlisted man in the German army to be decorated with the Knight's Cross. The episode revealed that,

German gunners firing a 15-millimeter field howitzer.

however weary and undersupplied the DAK was, the Eighth had not learned to coordinate a battle program and to direct it with a professional touch. Aware that his armor needed replacement and his troops needed training, Auchinleck closed down operations for the summer on July 27.

With the offensive postponed, veterans on both sides instinctively knew that preparations for the next few months could decide the fate of North Africa. If Rommel could regenerate his exhausted men, if he were supplied, if his tanks were replaced, and if the magic of his personality could inspire them to smash through El Alamein, then the long-sought prize on the Nile was his. But if Rommel and the Afrika Korps failed, they realized the awful consequences. For daily the Eighth grew stronger.

11
MONTGOMERY AND THE EIGHTH ARMY

SMOLDERING OVER the Eighth Army's failure to defeat the Afrika Korps, Churchill made his first inspection of the El Alamein front in early August to determine the reasons. The Commonwealth troops had retreated 800 miles during their "Gazala gallop," and the Nile was threatened by Rommel's next offensive. After conferring in Cairo, tramping along the lines under a broiling sun, and questioning officers and men, Churchill decided that the Eighth needed new leaders. He dismissed the luckless Auchinleck and replaced him with General Sir Harold Alexander as Britain's commander in chief of the Middle East. As field commander of the Eighth, the prime minister selected one of the most controversial soldiers in the British army—Lieutenant General Bernard Montgomery.

Churchill earnestly desired a mighty victory in North Africa. The recent months had been full of disasters. True, Britain itself was safe from invasion, the German attack on Stalingrad had been repulsed, and the United States was shipping troops and material to the British Isles. Yet Sevastopol on Russia's Black Sea had fallen to the Germans on July 1. Hitler's troops now could penetrate the Caucasus, invade neutral Turkey, and march to the oilfields of Iraq and Iran. Singapore—Britain's major naval base in the Far East—as well as Burma, Malaya, and the Dutch East Indies were overrun by the Japanese. Even India and Ceylon were threatened.

The ferocious Battle of the Atlantic continued. In July 1942, German submarines sank 600,000 tons of Allied shipping and by mid-August had destroyed another 400,000 tons. Malta, the most heavily bombed place in the war, was barely hanging on, for rarely did a merchant ship reach that besieged island. If Malta fell, and if Egypt were lost, the Mediterranean would become an Axis lake. On July 2 the prime minister barely won a vote of confidence in the British House of Commons concerning his conduct of the war. His political opposition and newspapers at home were highly critical of the string of defeats that marked the year's global fighting.

For the first time in the war, an Allied victory now seemed possible. Although Churchill neglected to give Auchinleck proper credit, the Eighth had blunted the DAK's thrust and had pinned it down at El Alamein. The Commonwealth army was growing stronger week by week, and El Alamein was the obvious place to demonstrate the abilities of the Eighth. In two naval engagements in the South Pacific (Coral Sea in May, Midway in June), the United States defeated Japanese fleets. Furthermore, Churchill and Roosevelt had conferred about opening a "second front" in an effort to assist their Russian ally. On July 25 the two leaders agreed on Operation Torch, a British-American amphibious invasion of French colonies in northwest Africa. Torch was scheduled for January 1943. If Allied forces could establish beachheads and then sweep over Morocco, Algeria, and Tunisia, and if the Eighth Army could defeat the Afrika Korps in Egypt, the Axis forces in North Africa could be trapped in Libya. Overruling pleas for planes, armor, and divisions to protect Commonwealth possessions in the Far East and to defend oil refineries in the Near East, Churchill staked his vision and prestige on Montgomery.

And who was this pink-cheeked, white-kneed, untanned soldier? When Montgomery arrived in Cairo on August 10, he was virtually unknown to the Eighth, except for his famous eccentricities. He was a small man, and he was not physically inspiring. Montgomery looked more like a clerk or bookkeeper than a military hero. Small and wiry, with a protruding nose and small head, he looked like a fierce terrier. He certainly did not seem like a man born to command. Montgomery was one of Britain's most widely discussed generals not because of his commendable but unspectacular military record, but because of his whims and peculiarities.

Montgomery was an excellent choice. Like Rommel, Montgomery had begun in the infantry. But unlike Rommel, Montgomery had witnessed the slaughter on the Western Front in World War I, which made him cautious about risking manpower. Again like Rommel, he had little money in his youth and few family connections to aid his career. He, too, rose in a class-conscious officer corps through toil, study, and commendable self-control. During the interwar years, he soldiered on three continents. Montgomery patiently prepared himself for his great moment of destiny, certain that it was God-ordained for him. He demonstrated endless energy, driving ambition, and an obsession with perfecting his talent for leadership.

In 1936 Montgomery had predicted that in the next European war, he would be the first British general to march into Berlin. Why his fellow officers failed to appreciate his genius —which Montgomery assumed was obvious—was puzzling to him. He certainly never doubted his own brilliance. By 1940 Montgomery was a divisional commander. In 1941 he impressed the general staff with his plan to repel a German invasion of England, and in 1942 he drew praise for his supervision of commando raids on the French coast. He had concentrated for decades on becoming a great military figure. Now in Egypt came his opportunity.

The fifty-five year old Montgomery was arrogant and quarrelsome. He was a professional warrior, totally dedicated to mastering the techniques of warfare. He was often ruthless to colleagues and unfair to subordinates. Except for a typical English interest in gardening, Montgomery was completely uninterested in matters unrelated to military affairs. After the death of his beloved wife in 1936, he became colder, more austere, and more detached from his fellow men. Montgomery could be charming to some comrades, but usually he was unapproachable in social affairs. He was cold and emotionally inaccessible. Obviously, Montgomery did not inspire warmth or friendship, nor did he intend to.

Montgomery refrained from smoking and drinking. He read the Bible daily and went to bed early. He scolded officers who dared to smoke in his presence; he once dismissed a brigadier general from duty for appearing fifteen minutes late for a conference. In 1941, in a unique order that was widely discussed in officers' mess, he ordered his entire staff to run cross-country three times a week to maintain physical fitness. No subordinate officer even dared to cough during Montgomery's lectures, for fear that "Monty" would immediately reprimand him in front of the class. "One had to be a bit of a cad [or scoundrel] to succeed in the army," Montgomery admitted. "I am a bit of a cad." He was rude and tactless. Professional competence in military matters and opportunities to demonstrate his brillance were uppermost in his life. Clearly, the caustic Montgomery had few pleasant personal characteristics. He certainly did not possess the appeal of Rommel.

Montgomery was particularly capable in three categories: handling logistics, delegating authority, and coordinating infantry, artillery, and engineers. Like a scientist, he analyzed strategic problems systematically to perfect his command into a well-lubricated machine. Unlike Rommel, who was willing to assume risks even when poorly supplied and perform daring end runs, Montgomery would never attack until his army was completely prepared, fully supplied, and provided with ample reserves of men and equipment. In contrast to Rommel, whose tendency was to devise a broad scheme and then improvise in battle day by day, Montgomery had a more methodical mind. He worked on a battle plan for months, he initiated a campaign exactly as he designed it, and he carried it through without deviation. Unlike Rommel, who led his troops into the heart of combat, Montgomery remained behind, but close to the lines, assuming that his commanders would carry out his orders.

Montgomery was deeply concerned with the morale of his troops and constantly roamed the campgrounds to determine the state of their welfare. His interest in the rank and file, however, was less humanitarian than military. He believed that spirited, disciplined, aggressive troops who were well fed, clothed, and sheltered were essential for victory. While Montgomery impressed his staff with his remarkable memory, his strategic insight, and his tight control of operations, he was not a daring general. In contrast to the Desert Fox, he was particularly weak in revising a battle scheme during a crisis. But the most common criticism of him in Cairo was that he was unfamiliar with tanks.

When Montgomery assumed command of the Eighth Army, he was keenly conscious of its morale problem. The army that Monty inherited had retreated since January from El Agheila to the outskirts of Cairo. The Eighth suffered from an inferiority complex because of its poor leadership, its supposed deficiency in weapons, its tactical errors in combat, and its inability to coordinate an attack. British officers worried about the endless defeats that the Eighth had sustained, the lack of preparations for the pending conflict that autumn, and the puzzle of how an army could be materially strong but spiritually weak. Montgomery realized that he had to restore the Eighth's confidence in itself and create an image of himself as a new type of British desert general—one who could win battles.

In two broad categories, Montgomery revitalized the Eighth —by overhauling his staff and by regenerating his troops. He began a drastic overhaul of the command structure by dismissing officers whose performances were not impressive, whose abilities he doubted, or who dared openly to question his strategy. He scrapped plans devised by Auchinleck for a withdrawal to the Nile, and he brought reinforcements from the delta to the front. He strengthened the El Alamein defenses with more wire and mines and increased the number of its strong points. Monty informed his startled staff that he would actually welcome an attack by Rommel. As a consequence of his attitude and activities, he gradually strengthened his commanders' resolve to hold El Alamein and to beat the Afrika Korps. But—unlike his predecessors who constantly quarreled with their commanders about tactics—he insisted that he would not tolerate differences of opinion concerning his orders. "I will take no bellyaching [his word for complaining]," Montgomery asserted. "The great point to remember is that we are going to finish with this chap Rommel once and for all." And in contrast to what had been chivalrous treatment of the enemy, Montgomery brought a new ferocity to the campaign. He repeatedly ordered his troops to "kill Germans where you find them."

Simultaneously, Montgomery realized that he had to create a public image that was quickly recognizable, one that his troops could identify as distinctive. Because he talked in a nasal, squeaky, high-pitched voice, he was not an inspiring speaker. Yet, Montgomery managed to overcome this deficiency. He developed an effective and confident manner of addressing soldiers, officers, and newspaper correspondents. To his own surprise, he developed a flair for publicity, and he attracted the imagination of civilians at home.

Montgomery used several techniques to demonstrate his individualism. He heard about a productive hen named Emma who daily laid an egg inside a Crusader tank. In honor of her achievements, Monty made the famous chicken an honorary regimental major. The Eighth needed a good joke. Henceforth, regiments had egg-laying contests with fowl purchased from Arabs. In dress, Montgomery discarded the traditional red-banded general's cap—which was always too big for his small head—and tried the wide-brimmed slouch hat of the Australians. To please the Commonwealth troops, he decorated his bush hat with their divisional badges. Montgomery deliberately displayed a casual appearance on the line, and his informal attire delighted the men. But Montgomery's pinched face looked somewhat ludicrous under the Australian hat, so he next wore the black beret of the tank men, adorning it with two armored brigade badges. He assumed a swaggering figure of confidence, wearing his famous beret and sweater, which became—like Rommel's goggles and binoculars—Montgomery's best known trademarks.

Montgomery was incredibly fussy ("fastidious" is a better word) about military regulations. He was annoyed that the hardened New Zealanders rarely bothered to salute him as he drove by their encampments. Montgomery complained about this discourtesy to Major General Bernard Freyberg, the battle-scarred New Zealand commander. Freyberg cheerfully informed Montgomery that his own men meant no disrespect, but that a tendency to avoid saluting was one of the national traits of troops from "Down Under" the equator. "Wave to them, sir," suggested Freyberg, "and they'll wave back." Thereafter Montgomery waved, and to his delight, the New Zealanders did wave back.

Gradually the legend of the tough, determined Montgomery grew. He continued to "sack" (or fire) inept subordinates. He insisted that officers be clean-shaven on duty (except for the permitted mustache) and that they appear punctually for meals. He tried to convince ground troops of their own abilities in combat. He demanded that tank commanders improve training techniques for their brigades. Monty inspired his men by refusing to run for cover when areas he was inspecting were shelled by enemy fire. His so-called jokes at officers' clubs were pitiful attempts to be funny by a humorless man, but at least he tried to relax his colleagues. In addressing his troops, he was more direct and skillful. "The infantry must be prepared to kill," he bluntly informed them, "and to continue doing so over a prolonged period." By daily visits to the front, by moving his headquarters to an RAF airfield near the line, by frequent discussions with divisional commanders, Montgomery slowly shaped the ailing Eighth into fighting trim. Monty's drive, his

Field Marshall Bernard Montgomery posing by a Grant tank as a shell explodes behind him.

attempts to improve morale, and his sense of confidence that Rommel could be beaten inspired the rank and file.

Montgomery thus rebuilt the Eighth into a force that seemed to be capable of grappling with the next enemy thrust. Beyond the defensive aspects of his planning, he also prepared to mount his own offensive, once the DAK was hurled back. To beat Rommel at his own game and to match the mobility of the Afrika Korps, Montgomery created a separate corps of three tank brigades and one motorized infantry brigade. The brave but foolhardy armored charges of the past were over. Henceforth, tank men, gunners, and ground troops would co-ordinate, and armor would fight to the end to protect riflemen. Montgomery also devised a novel technique for desert combat. He planned close support by low-flying planes for his divisions. The RAF practiced "carpet-bombing," dropping explosives in precise formation at low altitudes by day on concentrated areas. At night, the pilots were prepared to continue the bombing but also to drop thousands of flares to light up the sky for British artillery. As a result of Monty's dynamic leadership, Major General Sir H. Kippenberger, the leader of the Fifth New Zealand Brigade, said that "the morale of the whole army went up incredibly."

But the acid test of leadership, training, and tactical ability comes in combat. Now the first trial of the supposedly improved Eighth would occur at the dominating topographical feature of the area. Five miles behind the El Alamein Line lay the five-mile-long ridge of Alam el Halfa. Here the DAK and the Eighth would clash in a bloody contest.

The Eighth seemed in good shape—in material, intelligence, and geographic location. For weeks there had been a massive infusion of men, supplies, and equipment. The RAF was ready with 530 planes. The artillery had 84 of the new six-pound antitank guns, a match for the 88. Montgomery's force numbered 195,000 troops, almost double the size of Rommel's command. The Commonwealth forces had over 1,000 tanks: about 700 on the line, 200 in repair, and 100 in transit. Up front were 200 Shermans and 210 new Grants, built in the United States. The Grant weighed 36 tons, had 62-millimeter armor, traveled at a speed of 25 miles an hour, and fired a high-velocity shell from its 75-millimeter cannon. It was superior to the Mark III and to the Mark IV, but not to the Mark IV Special.

Montgomery's intelligence section, alerted by Ultra, deduced that Rommel would attack during August's full moon somewhere in the south, probably near Alam el Halfa. British intelligence monitored Rommel's signals with speed and regularity. Montgomery's staff knew that Rommel was dubious about success in the pending battle. They also knew about his quarrels with Rome and Berlin, about the state of his health, and about the time and place of the coming assault. Intelligence, in Cairo, could predict even the point of attack. Rommel had two choices: he could try to hammer his way through the cluttered mine field north of Ruweisat Ridge, or he could push around the southern tip of the El Alamein Line. Only in a swift, disciplined maneuver or a wide sweep did the DAK have the advantage in tactics, experience, and leadership over the Eighth.

With respect to terrain, the Eighth seemed secure. North of Ruweisat Ridge were ground troops—Indians, South Africans, Australians—well protected by mines, stout defense points, and heavy artillery. Just south of Ruweisat Ridge was the Second New Zealand Division, also behind a sea of mines. The Qattara Depression effectively blocked Rommel's familiar long right hook. Even if Rommel punched a hole through the southern sector, he would be confronted by Alam el Halfa Ridge, which, properly defended, could prevent an Axis breakthrough.

Montgomery devised his own "cauldron" for Rommel. To slow the DAK's penetration from the south, Montgomery placed additional mine fields there. An armored brigade and motorized troops were to fight briefly and then retire slowly eastward. Once it entered the trap, the Afrika Korps would be exposed to pressure in whatever direction it took. Montgomery covered all gaps with explosives, kept his armor flexible, and doubled the number of men and guns on the ridge. If Rommel tried to run south and then west of the ridge he would encounter the powerful Seventh Armored Division. If he swung north, he would be blocked not only by Alam el Halfa but by the Tenth Armored Division with its 210 tanks. If he swung west of the ridge, his Panzers would encounter the Twenty-second and Twenty-third Armored Brigades, in addition to motorized troops and the Forty-fourth Infantry on the ridge. The trick was for the British Seventh Armored in the south to harass the Panzers and then lure them to an ambush just west of the ridge. Here at its strongest point tanks waited hull down, and defenses bristled with antitank guns.

Except for the Australians and New Zealanders, Montgomery realized that his infantrymen were generally inferior to Rommel's and that his artillerymen were still learning to concentrate their fire. His armor could not match Rommel's devious pattern of feints and thrusts. Hence, Montgomery planned a static defense. He selected the battleground and prepared to repulse the DAK. Outnumbering the Axis forces, he planned by sheer manpower to pin them down and destroy them piece by piece. Even if portions of the Eighth were surrounded, he proclaimed, his men were to fight and to kill Germans. He convinced his troops that surrender was unthinkable. For the first time in North Africa, Rommel's moves were fully comprehended by a general capable of directing a correct deployment of troops, and one with enough equipment to smother the enemy. Now the Eighth awaited the onslaught.

As Rommel prepared to attack, supply problems again perplexed him. The key was Malta, which again had a profound effect on the action in Egypt. Hitler had postponed the assault on the island, and, consequently, its planes and ships continued to smash convoys destined for the DAK. By the date of his offensive, Rommel had only one-third of the supplies he needed.

Rommel had only 350 planes. He commanded 104,000 troops, of which one-half were from Italian divisions of varying quality. He possessed 200 German and 327 Italian tanks, against Montgomery's total of 1,029. He could depend on only 20 of the lethal 88s. Rommel was not only heavily outnumbered but also physically unprepared for his next great adventure. Sick with jaundice—a typical desert disease—and with intestinal disorders, Rommel was so weary that he could barely climb into a tank. Yet, one more effort, some luck, and the usual enemy fumbling could make him master of the Nile.

At 2200 on August 30, he feinted at the center of Ruweisat Ridge. Then, predictably, he tried his familiar scheme of leading mobile units around the southern tip of the El Alamein Line just above the Qattara Depression. But once again, he gave his strike force of 443 tanks too ambitious a timetable. He expected his men to sweep south in a great circle, clear the mine fields by dawn, and then push beyond Alam el Halfa. By morning, he anticipated that his Panzers would be thirty miles from their starting line, well beyond Alam el Halfa and near the coast, where his force would cut off the Eighth's railroad. He expected the usual slow British response, numerous gaps in enemy mine fields, and a swift drive to the shoreline before the enemy armor could coordinate. But there were many uncertainties. He could succeed only if he caught the enemy off guard, if his intelligence about enemy positions was correct, if the Luftwaffe supplied him with fuel, and if British armored brigades separated to attack his Panzers.

But his plan was doomed from the start. Even before Rommel launched his risky operation, the RAF had detected the Axis assembly area, penetrated the Axis fighter screen, and plastered the Panzers with "round-the-clock" bombing that continued for days. The terrain around the edge of the line was more difficult than Rommel had envisioned. Seas of loose sand slowed his armor, and devilish mine fields covered a much larger area than he had anticipated. The enemy armored brigade and motorized troops that the Panzers first encountered resisted fiercely, causing another delay. Then thick dust storms caused some Panzer regiments to become separated. So fierce was the opposition that at 0800 the next day, Rommel nearly called off the offensive.

Yet soon after, his sappers managed to clear the mines, and after knocking out the Fourth Armored Brigade and the Seventh Motor Brigade, his Panzers were free to move eastward. But Rommel was now hours behind schedule. So, prevented from bypassing Alam el Halfa, he cut down the destination points to the east by twenty miles, wheeled his force due north, and rammed right into the Twenty-second Armored, which waited just south of Alam el Halfa.

But Rommel had wheeled the Afrika Korps almost due north much earlier than his commanders expected, and his force plunged into the most heavily defended sector of Alam el Halfa. To their surprise, the Panzers encountered fierce tank resistance, scores of British antitank guns concealed along the ridge, and constant bombardment from the sky.

Badly mauled by evening, the Afrika Korps retired south to

regroup and refuel, badly shaken by being repulsed and outwitted at Alam el Halfa. The Eighth Army's hidden artillery and effective use of antitank guns had been surprise enough, but a new threat on the battlefield was the Grant tank whose powerful shells ripped huge, jagged holes in dozens of Rommel's tanks. Yet the major factor in the defeat of the DAK at Alam el Halfa was Montgomery's use of air power. The RAF flew five hundred sorties that day, and the American flying squadrons gave support. The combined air forces dropped tons and tons of bombs on the DAK not only during the day but also at night, when the formations continued to dump their loads, along with thousands of flares. This new fear of being constantly blocked, shelled, and bombed increased the Germans' sense of helplessness. Its regiments were scattered, and some units were without ammunition.

By September 1 Montgomery knew that he had guessed Rommel's plan correctly. The slaughter went on, but with a drastic change. The skies belonged to the RAF, and the Luftwaffe was unable to transport fuel. The terrain was filled with burning hulks of vehicles. The air was hot, arid, and saturated with sand. The Panzers continued to absorb the punishment for hours, pounded by tanks, guns, and planes. Rommel narrowly missed death when a shell exploded just as he jumped into a trench. As the brutal pounding at Alam el Halfa continued, the DAK seemed almost passive, taking its punishment and losing its initiative. At noon on September 2, realizing that his attack was a failure, Rommel began a cautious withdrawal. The decisive event was the news that three more Italian tankers had been sunk off Tobruk on September 1. It was no longer possible to sustain the operation. Rommel's grand plan sputtered to an inglorious end.

To Rommel's surprise, Montgomery did not pursue. The British general was impressed with the Panzer skills and their 88s. His own armor was badly damaged, and he was unprepared for a counterattack. By September 6 the Axis troops were back behind their lines, licking their wounds. The men of the Afrika Korps realized that they had nearly been defeated, that they had been granted only a breathing space. Unless supplies increased significantly and unless Rommel's luck improved, the DAK's next battle could end in a major defeat.

Losses at Alam el Halfa were about equal in men, guns, and tanks. Back at headquarters on September 4, Rommel took off his boots for the first time in a week. Badly in need of medical treatment, Rommel waited until September 23 to fly home for hospitalization in Germany. His temporary replacement at El Alamein was General Georg Stumme, a veteran of the Russian front. Yet Rommel's men were not worried. Rommel— their chief, their idol, their father figure—promised to return within a few weeks. As usual, he would think of something to save the day, regardless of the odds.

For the Eighth Army, Alam el Halfa was particularly important, for it was a psychological victory. True, the Afrika Korps had merely been checked, not destroyed, but it was clear to Montgomery's men that his meticulous planning for the battle had paid off. The pilots, ground troops, artillery, and motorized infantry had fought well. Only the armor still lacked the teamwork necessary to defeat the Panzers. Consequently, as tank training was intensified to overcome this deficiency, the Eighth prepared for the next round with more confidence in their commander. And Montgomery, never a modest fellow, boasted: "Egypt has been saved. It is now a mathematical certainty that I will eventually destroy Rommel."

While the opposing forces tried to determine the enemy's intentions, another clock was ticking overseas: Operation Torch. Torch was a risky operation involving landings by three separate task forces on the coast of French northwest Africa. The anticipated beachhead for the Western Task Force was Casablanca in Morocco. The target for the Central Task Force was Oran, and for the East Force, Algiers. The Western Task Force, which was to sail from United States ports in late 1943, was composed of American ships and troops. The Anglo-

American center and eastern forces were to sail from the United Kingdom, escorted by the Royal Navy.

The commanders of Torch were not confident about the projected landings. This undertaking was the largest amphibious attempt ever mounted over such long distances. The Battle of the Atlantic was still being waged, and German submarines lurked in the dark waters. Yet the Allies were willing to risk sending 112 transport ships, laden with troops, and 75 naval vessels from America, along with 240 transports and 94 British naval ships from England, right through the formidable U-boat packs that were concentrated off the British Isles and Gibraltar.

The planners of Operation Torch faced many uncertainties and imponderables, including the tricky matter of determining the safest landings in unpredictable winds and tides. The potential gains for this daring project were clearly worthwhile. If Torch proceeded smoothly, the Allies could occupy key cities and airfields in two French colonies. And while these areas were being taken, the Allies could push out from Algeria to capture ports in Tunisia before Axis troops arrived.

Torch was an enormous gamble, but if the operation was successful the advantages for the Allies would be enormous. A "second front" could be opened in Africa, and from Tunisia the Allies could invade Sicily, Sardinia, and Italy itself. In September, still unaware of the Allied strategy, Rommel and the Afrika Korps were in danger of being trapped in Libya between two Allied armies. Rommel had to win decisively at El Alamein.

12
EL ALAMEIN

As THE echoes of Alam el Halfa faded away, Rommel faced several problems at El Alamein. He could not retreat for several reasons: the lack of fuel, the shortage of transport, and the opposition of Hitler and Mussolini to a withdrawal. Without a wide southern flank for maneuver, he forced Montgomery to a battle of attrition. No natural obstacles impeded the Eighth, nor could Rommel construct bastions without any rock, steel, and concrete. He had no alternative but to make his position impregnable by building a fortress in the sand.

Rommel suspected that Montgomery would attack him between Ruweisat and Miteirya ridges. To minimize British air and artillery superiority, he designed a system of defenses to prevent enemy penetrations. The Afrika Korps was fortunate that Rommel was an infantryman who knew siegecraft, trench arrangements, and mechanical devices for mine fields. Before he left for the hospital on September 22, he perfected methods to repulse the enemy.

He did not have enough men, guns, tanks, and barbed wire to cover forty miles of sand, ridges, and depressions, so he built a double belt of defenses, about five miles deep running north and south. The first line, two thousand yards wide, was manned by infantry outposts. It was filled with antitank mines and mortars, machine guns, trenches, and blockhouses. About two thousand yards back was the second belt of three thousand yards, filled with explosives, light artillery, and antitank guns. Behind these lethal carpets was the third line of resistance—a gun line held by tanks and 88s. The DAK would inflict enormous casualties on the Eighth if it intruded on Rommel's killing zones.

Most of the mines were the flat, black Teller mines rigged to explode under the weight of a vehicle. They could demolish a truck or blow off a tank's track. Among these devices were "S" mines, shaped like tin cans and designed to destroy the running infantry. These smaller mines were triggered by booby traps. Their explosions sprang three feet into the air, scattering lethal steel pellets that maimed and killed ground troops. Not only were these mines cleverly concealed in the ground, but many were rigged to ignite other mines or the firing pins of hidden aircraft bombs. All these devices—about 250,000 of them—were planted in Rommel's "Devil's Garden."

The mines and the defense zones scattered within the belts gave cover. Rommel also needed to prevent enemy intrusions through these lines. About 54,000 Italian troops held the area, but some Italian units could bend and break under pressure. So the Desert Fox took the risk of "sandwiching" his German infantry among the Italians in order to plug gaps at weak sectors and mount counterattacks. The difficulty for Rommel was that he would be unable to use his best riflemen at critical points. Rommel also had to divide his Panzers. He kept the Twenty-first Panzer and Ariete divisions in the north, but he had to deploy the Fifteenth Panzer and Littorio armor thirty miles to the south.

Rommel's greatest worry was gasoline. He needed three hundred tons of fuel daily just to sustain his army and six hundred tons for every day of battle. Yet, during September, the Allies had sunk virtually every Italian tanker headed for Libya. On the eve of battle, Rommel's command had fuel for only four days, ammunition for nine days, bread for three weeks, and no fresh fruit or vegetables.

As the battle approached, Rommel had 104,000 troops

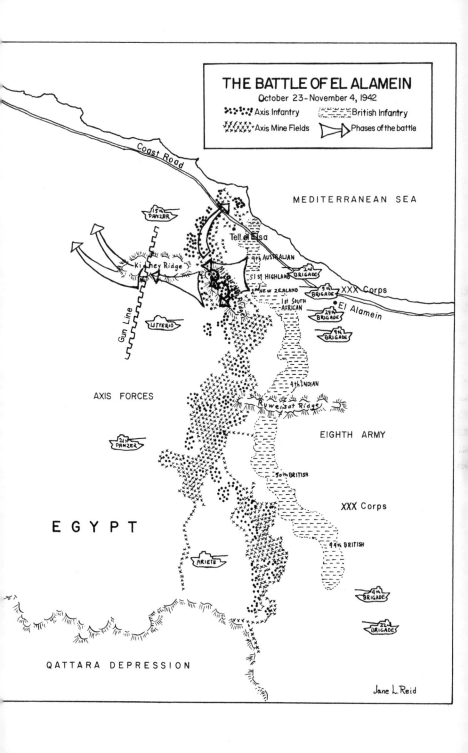

THE BATTLE OF EL ALAMEIN

October 23-November 4, 1942

- Axis Infantry
- Axis Mine Fields
- British Infantry
- Phases of the battle

Coast Road

MEDITERRANEAN SEA

15th PANZER

Tell el Eisa

Kidney Ridge

9th AUSTRALIAN

51st HIGHLAND

2nd BRIGADE

NEW ZEALAND

5th BRIGADE

XXX Corps

1st SOUTH AFRICAN

El Alamein

24th BRIGADE

Gun Line

LITTORIO

9th BRIGADE

AXIS FORCES

4th INDIAN

Ruweisat Ridge

EIGHTH ARMY

21st PANZER

50th BRITISH

XXX Corps

E G Y P T

44th BRITISH

ARIETE

4th BRIGADE

21st BRIGADE

QATTARA DEPRESSION

Jane L. Reid

(half of them German), 500 tanks (half of them German), 500 artillery pieces, and 800 antitank guns. Montgomery had 195,000 men, over 1,000 cruiser tanks, 900 artillery pieces, and 1,450 antitank guns. In planes, the Allies outnumbered the Axis; the skies belonged to the British and American air forces.

General Stumme and General Ritter Wilhelm von Thoma, his second in command, sensed an attack for late October, but they were uncertain of the direction of the enemy's thrust. Confident that his material resources would overwhelm Rommel, Montgomery refused to hurry his preparations for the autumn offensive. Churchill was impatient for an attack in September, not only to defeat Rommel but also to relieve Malta, to impress the French forces in northwest Africa, and to prepare for the Torch landings now scheduled for November 8. But Montgomery was stubborn. He refused to move until his army was ready.

As the morale and the training of the Eighth improved, Montgomery's staff tried to fool the Desert Fox by deceptive devices. In a set-piece battle like El Alamein, with little room to maneuver, the attacker attempts to deceive the defender about the timing and point of assault. Montgomery executed his plan with great attention to detail, designing it in such a way that Rommel would be tricked into thinking that the southern sector was the target and that the attack would occur during the November full moon.

The British perfected the art of duping their enemy by a variety of tricks to conceal depots, weapons, vehicles, and troop concentrations. Montgomery planned to strike just north of the center in the most heavily defended sector. But to fool the German generals into believing that the attack was coming from the south, the British tried some ingenious stunts.

Because netting (traditionally used in Europe to conceal weapons) was too dark to hide equipment from enemy aircraft, the camouflage experts experimented with hues, colors, and fabrics to hide tanks and guns and to suggest the existence of false areas of concentration. The specialists of "A Force," as the camouflage group was known, manufactured wooden guns, built phony mess halls and barracks, set up false dumps and entire tented towns near the southern lines. They built false roads, make-believe airfields, and counterfeit forward bases. "A Force" learned to simulate buildings, trenches, and hangars by painting dark shadows on the ground. One classic case of deception was the construction of a fake railroad track, complete with dummy cars and locomotives built at half-size, some ten miles ahead of the real depot where equipment was nightly unloaded. The Luftwaffe bombed the fake terminal every time.

The British also played games with real guns, tanks, and trucks. Armored tracks on the sand were covered over by special teams to conceal the routing of motorized brigades. Wooden frames were placed over tanks to suggest a depot full of boxes or trucks, not mobile armor. Some 700 dummy trucks were fitted over real tanks in this manner. Another trick was to move armor and trucks by daylight. At night, phony vehicles replaced them while the real vehicles were moved to a secret location. Guns were concealed by digging in the sand, lowering the artillery into the pits, covering them with trucks, and, on the eve of the offensive, hauling the guns out. Some 360 pieces of artillery were covered in this manner.

The Eighth's most successful visual deception was the construction of a dummy pipeline that extended twenty miles southward. Without sufficient metal pipe to complete the project, "A Force" strung together gasoline cans to suggest a meandering waterline, or so it appeared to Axis pilots. The "pipeline" was then covered with sand like a real one. The gasoline cans were removed at night to continue construction of the false water supply farther south. The entire trick was complete with fake pump houses, reservoirs, and maintenance facilities. It was designed to indicate completion by early November.

Along with such imaginative tricks, the Eighth's communication centers sent messages to and from nonexistent units, contrived new locations for imaginary divisions, and faked the movements of actual brigades. The deception was so successful that Axis intelligence failed to detect a buildup bigger than anyone had anticipated: two entire divisions, 150 tanks, 240 guns, and 7,500 tons of fuel. That an attack was pending was obvious. But the date, the direction, and the degree of strength involved in the assault were well-guarded secrets.

The length and depth of the Devil's Garden presented a challenge to the Allies. They would have to breach the mine fields, maintain an impetus through the openings, and reach the far side of the belts before the Panzers could rally and block. The burden would fall on the infantry and the sappers clearing corridors for the tanks and other vehicles. But to assist them, and to throw the enemy off balance, Montgomery coordinated his air and artillery power.

To wreck the enemy's defense posts in the Devil's Garden, and to disrupt his communications, Montgomery planned the greatest British barrage since World War I. Over nine hundred guns would "soften" the Axis lines. With the skies cleared and the Axis defenses pulverized, Montgomery intended to punch two main channels into the northern area over a ten-mile front. The task was assigned to the Thirtieth Corps commanded by Lieutenant General Oliver Leese whose four divisions of infantry and sappers would eliminate nests of Axis ground troops and would neutralize mine-free corridors. A passage in the north was to be cleared of mines by the Ninth Australian Division and the Fifty-first Highlanders, while the Second New Zealand and the First South African divisions cleared passes farther south. Once these routes had been opened, the Tenth Armored Corps under Lieutenant Herbert Lumsden would push through the belts. Once the Tenth reached Kidney Ridge and Miteirya Ridge, British armor would attack Rommel's Panzers and then crack his gun screen.

Ten miles farther south the British would create a third opening, but the terrain here was difficult for tanks. Actually it was a diversionary effort by the Thirtieth Corps under Lieutenant General Brian Horrocks commanding the Seventh Armored Division, the Fiftieth Infantry Division, and the Free French Brigade. This feint was intended to pin down Rommel's armor in the south. Horrocks was ordered not to sustain heavy losses. There were some interesting aspects in Montgomery's battle plan. First, unlike his predecessors, he was deliberately attacking Rommel's strongest sector. Second, he was following traditional tank doctrine by attempting to defeat Rommel's tanks and then crush his infantry.

But during the September training, Montgomery wondered whether his plan was too risky. His infantry commanders doubted that their men could clear the mines on schedule, and armored commanders were equally dubious that the ground troops could open up corridors according to Montgomery's tight schedule. Thus, on October 6, just two weeks before the offensive, Montgomery modified his original plan and gave the Tenth Corps armor a more realistic objective—two miles beyond the mine belts, not five miles as he had originally planned. Then, instead of using the tanks as his main fist and having them hold off the Panzers, he placed a greater burden on the infantry. The coordination of the air and artillery bombardments was unchanged. But Montgomery now ordered the Thirtieth Corps of ground troops to destroy Rommel's infantry in the Devil's Garden while the Tenth Corps armor passed through to hold off Rommel's tanks on the far side of the mine fields. In a decision that was a fundamental reverse of standard desert tank concepts—which called for destroying the enemy armor first and then smashing the infantry—Montgomery turned the process around. He would destroy the enemy ground troops first in the Devil's Garden, then Rommel's armor, and finally his gun line. Thus, by a simple but vital adjustment in his blueprint, Montgomery decided that when his tanks reached the west side of the second mine belt, the armor would stand fast and repel the Panzers, while his infantry eliminated the Axis soldiers in the Devil's Garden. This was Montgomery's final adjustment to his battle plan. But even this more limited set of objectives would be difficult to attain if the Afrika Korps fought well.

On the night of October 23 the Eighth was tense with readiness. Military police guided tanks to their start lines. Not since Operation Crusader had expectations of victory been so high. As usual, Montgomery retired early. He gave orders not to be disturbed until morning, read a detective story, and turned off his lantern at 2100.

At 2140 on October 23, the Allied artillery opened the offensive with a cataract of noise unknown before in the Western Desert. Gun barrels glowed with heat as perspiring gunners rammed shell after shell into the breeches and ignored the concussions that rocked their eardrums. Nearly deaf from the man-made thunder that lasted fifteen minutes, the artillerymen found their thick gloves burned through by the red-hot gun muzzles. Some nine hundred rounds a minute burst at Axis strong points, throwing up geysers of sand, blasting huge chunks of wire, and detonating mines. Blockhouses collapsed, dugouts and trenches crumbled, and thousands of mines exploded under the impact. The air was filled with stones and shell splinters. The sand reflected the red glow of the detonations, and a pale moon illuminated the battlefield.

The four assault divisions of Thirtieth Corps made progress by 0100, reaching the edge of the first mine belt. They were scheduled to be through both belts by 0245, closely followed by the tanks. The riflemen, bayonets fixed, moved three yards apart, about fifty yards a minute. But they encountered innumerable delays in finding paths through the Devil's Garden. After the creeping barrages, the advances resumed in stages. But opposition became stronger, and dozens of unconnected skirmishes occurred in a nightmare of confusion. The barrage had churned up banks of dust. Even in moonlight, visibility was limited to a few yards. Dust thickened like a choking, suffocating blanket. The grand design of the plan was almost forgotten as the infantry stumbled through the night, groping for the right direction, hoping not to step on the wire prongs of the lethal "S" mines.

The sappers had an equally dangerous task. Some men located mines with the unreliable electronic detectors, but the majority of the devices were found by carefully probing in the soil with bayonets, steel rods, or bare hands. The second group gently removed the defused explosives from the sand and stacked them in long piles. The third group placed white tape, and red and green lights to mark the corridors. Sappers were supposed to clear lanes about twenty-four feet wide to allow two tanks to pass abreast. But, moving along at about two hundred yards an hour, they were unable to remove the mines quickly; their pace was far behind Montgomery's ambitious timetable for clearing the corridors by dawn. Thousands of mines exploded, and their unfortunate victims lay sprawled and screaming on the sand.

Within a few hours, the advance of Lumsden's armor became a nightmare. Only some New Zealand infantry reached the slopes of Miteirya Ridge by dawn, while the troops of the other three infantry divisions were one to two miles behind their objectives. The tanks made hardly any headway and were enmeshed in the Devil's Garden. Movement on the narrow and congested corridors was maddeningly slow, and it grew more erratic hour by hour as the men fell hours behind schedule. All of Lumsden's fears were realized. Although the First Armored Division managed to position some tanks beyond the second belt by sunrise, the unlucky Tenth Armored's 250 tanks churned away helplessly, foot-deep in dust, trapped in crammed passages. German planes appeared, dropping flares and bombs on the helpless vehicles. The horizon became an enormous crackling furnace, illuminating the landscape for miles and making the shattered Tenth Armored an easy German target. A few tanks of the Tenth Armored managed to nose their way to the far side, but immediately they encountered another mine sector, the awesome power of 88s, and well-concealed Panzers. The hoped-for rapid advance slowed to a crawl, and by dawn the armor was unable to attain its goal of carving a salient ten miles wide and five miles deep. Commonwealth infantry fought desperately to subdue numerous Axis posts that remained intact in the Devil's Garden. British armor was pinned down under murderous fire. The majority of the tanks were packed behind the slow-moving infantry and sappers.

In the far south, Horrocks and the Tenth Corps made a diversionary attack and penetrated the first mine belt, but they were unable to break into the second. Yet the Eighth had exerted a sufficient threat here to keep the Twenty-first Panzer and Littorio divisions tied down. By noon on October 24 no major breakthrough had occurred. Reviewing his limited progress, Montgomery nevertheless decided to continue the pressure another day. He hoped that the Fifty-first Infantry could reach Kidney Ridge and that the Tenth Armored could fight its way out of its smoking corridor.

On the Axis side, the intensity of the opening artillery barrage was a surprise. The reaction to the infantry assault on the Devil's Garden was delayed by the shelling, which jammed communication lines. Puzzled about the enemy's intentions, Stumme needed fresh information. His headquarters had been wrecked by British artillery, and he had lost contact with several field commanders. Unable to visualize the battle, Stumme drove to the line in his car. In the confusion, his driver headed right into a company of Australian machine gunners. Stumme's chauffeur quickly turned the vehicle to escape the withering fire as Stumme tried to leap from the car. But Stumme could only cling to the door of the speeding, swirling vehicle, and he toppled to the ground, dead of a heart attack.

Thoma had immediately assumed command of the Axis forces and notified Berlin of the attack. Ordered out of his hospital bed by Hitler, Rommel arrived by plane at El Alamein on the evening of October 25. After studying the reports on fuel supplies, tank losses, and troop casualties, Rommel realized that the partial breaching of the Devil's Garden eliminated his

A German Panzer crewman surrenders to British infantry at El Alamein.

hope for a stalemated battle. Unless he could repulse Montgomery's armor, his "Africans" would be destroyed by overwhelming odds.

Meanwhile on the afternoon of October 24, the British Fifty-first Division managed to open the northern corridor as far as Kidney Ridge, and by nightfall two Allied armored brigades were on its slopes. But in one of the most destructive tank battles of the desert war, thirty-one Sherman tanks of the Tenth Armored were hit by 88s and lit up like candles. Other tank brigades were still stalled in the mine fields, particularly in the southern corridor. Axis artillery, Luftwaffe flares, and bombs rained on the Eighth Armored Brigade and prevented it from moving. Even some tanks that got through the Devil's Garden were exposed to Panzers and antitank guns at Miteirya Ridge.

Leese and Lumsden wanted to halt the attack. They insisted that victory was not worth the cost in lives. The two took the unprecedented step of waking up Montgomery at 0330 on October 25 to urge him to terminate the assault. Montgomery listened politely to his worried commanders. But he was stubborn and insisted that the armor fight its way out, regardless of the loss thus far of one hundred tanks and six thousand men. Montgomery could accept heavy casualties, for he still had nine hundred tanks in operation, and the morale of his infantry was still high. His decision to continue to fight a losing battle marked the turning point of El Alamein. Unlike previous British commanders, Montgomery was willing to tolerate enormous bloodshed to hammer the DAK into oblivion.

By late morning that day, the Tenth Armored had managed to extricate itself from the southern corridor and approach Miteirya Ridge. It found few positions there for concealment, however, so the tank brigades withdrew to the east side of the ridge to avoid enemy fire. Most of the ground troops were still battling in the Devil's Garden, much of the armor was still trapped there, and the few tank brigades that emerged from the mine fields found it impossible to create the defensive shield that Montgomery intended. With tank losses of 250 for the Eighth Army by October 26, the battle was stalled. In fact, even though the Fifteenth Panzer Division had lost 90 of its 120 tanks, the struggle was gradually tilting toward Rommel's favor. Montgomery had to find a new sector and exploit it quickly.

Fortunately for him, reports of fighting near the coast were more encouraging. Since October 24, the Ninth Australian Division had been driving toward a slight elevation, termed Point 29, just south of the coastal road. With excellent tank and artillery support and efficient mine clearance, Morshead's men had captured the position by nightfall on October 25. Point 29 gave the Eighth a good observation location overlooking the northern edge of the line and opened an area for an advance. This unexpected gain gave Montgomery the opportunity to shift the weight of his offensive farther northward while he still applied pressure with the Fifty-first at Kidney Ridge and the New Zealanders and South Africans at Miteirya Ridge.

At the same time, Rommel was worried about the precision of the enemy's bombardment and about the continued pressure in the corridors. The Trento Division fought valiantly, but it was shattered. The crack German 164th Regiment was eliminated. The Fifteenth Panzer and Ariete divisions were struggling to prevent enemy brigades from breaking out near the ridges. Under the circumstances, Rommel had to recover Point 29. His first attack on the twenty-foot rise by Italian infantry was repulsed by RAF bombing and Australian artillery. Needing armor from the south, Rommel ordered the Twenty-first Panzer and Littorio divisions from their positions thirty miles away to mount a counteroffensive at Point 29. Now, desperate to hold the ridges, he also ordered the Ninetieth Light and Trieste divisions out of reserve to reinforce his coastal sector. Rommel was now concentrating his Panzers. But it was a dangerous game. Montgomery could renew the attack in the far south, in the Devil's Garden, or at Point 29.

On October 27 Rommel thrust at Kidney Ridge with the Twenty-first Panzer and Ninetieth Light. But this time he underestimated the enemy's determination to resist and overestimated the ability of his troops to attack. Short of fuel, blasted by artillery and concealed antitank guns, Rommel lost thirty-seven tanks in the attempt. Under the determined Montgomery, a transformation of the Eighth Army had occurred. The British and Commonwealth troops were prepared to retaliate against the heretofore dreaded Panzers. And the Panzers, as tough and expert as they were, no longer had the weapon superiority against Sherman tanks and 105-millimeter guns. As Rommel explained the incident, "a murderous British fire struck into our ranks and our attack was soon brought to a halt by an immensely powerful antitank defense. . . . We suffered considerable losses and were obliged to withdraw."

Meanwhile Montgomery performed a unique operation in handling his reserves. He pulled the Seventh Armored and Fiftieth divisions out of the south and brought the Second New Zealand Division in from the Devil's Garden (replacing it with the Fourth Indian Division) to create a new strike force. Aware of this new buildup, on October 28 Rommel ordered his Panzers on the defensive at Kidney Ridge and Point 29. The dependable Ninetieth Light repulsed the Ninth Australian near Tell el Eisa, but the fight took a terrible toll in manpower. Montgomery's policy of waging brutal attrition to wear down his enemy was gradually succeeding. When Rommel learned that three more Italian tankers had been sunk off Libya, he prepared a new defense line to the west. By October 29 he was so pessimistic that he admitted in a letter to his wife that "I have not much hope left." Yet Rommel knew that a sudden retreat by his armor and motorized troops would mean abandoning his ground troops. To leave his comrades behind was unthinkable for Rommel. Thus, even with his line bending and buckling, he was determined to hold.

At this moment, Montgomery made another shift. Inasmuch as the Australians' advance along the coast had stalled, Montgomery switched the pressure of his offensive back to the ridges. Then, when he discovered that Rommel had moved all his German armor and best German infantry to Point 29, Montgomery likewise shifted a portion of his force at an objective about five miles south of his original target. The attacks at Kidney Ridge and along the coast would continue, but the new emphasis would come at the "hinge," where the German troops of the Ninetieth Light and the Italian troops of the Trento Division linked. Here was the suspected weak point in Rommel's line, and here was where Montgomery thrust his reserve force of armor and infantry. As the moon paled on October 29, Montgomery's objective was to open a new gap four thousand yards wide and five thousand yards deep. Preceded by an intensive artillery barrage, the Second New Zealand and the Fifty-first Infantry made a breach so that tanks could pass through by dawn. The target for the armor, four miles beyond the point of exploitation, was Rommel's last defense line—the concentration of Axis artillery on the north–south road called the Rahman Track.

The breakthrough came at 0600 on November 2. Pounded by air, artillery, and tank fire, the German and Italian troops retired from their last mined area. The dam finally burst. Led by the Ninth Armored Brigade, the Commonwealth troops lunged forward to Miteirya Ridge, creeping one hundred yards every three minutes under a heavy barrage. By dawn the Ninth Armored had reached the Rahman Track. There the unit was blasted by 88s and lost seventy of its ninety-four tanks. Though the Axis gun line had been fractured, it was still not broken. Losses continued to be enormous on both sides, but Montgomery insisted that the attack continue as the brutal slugging match for the mastery of Egypt went on. Pillars of oily smoke rose from ditched British armor silhouetted against a blood red sky. The First Armored Brigade was slower to emerge from the congested gaps behind the infantry, but, luckily, it was in position to repel the Panzer attack and to dent another sector of the Rahman Track.

Rommel had been deceived. Certain that Montgomery would concentrate on Point 29, he had ordered Thoma to hit it with every available tank. But when dawn came, he realized that Montgomery was hitting farther south than he had anticipated—right at Thoma's gun line. Rommel radioed Thoma to deploy southward, but hours were lost by the sudden change of direction. Not until noon did Thoma's force emerge at the Rahman Track. There the Panzers fought desperately, losing 117 tanks, to stem the tide of battle. By now, the Eighth had an advantage over the Afrika Korps of nearly twenty to one in tanks alone.

Rommel's Fifteenth and Twenty-first Panzers hit the British brigades from both sides. Men from the 104th Panzer Grenadiers even used their rifles against the steady streams of British tanks that poured through. Some Germans in sheer desperation hurled grenades at the metal monsters. Although another seventy British tanks were knocked out in the action, numerous holes were made in the Rahman Track. By nightfall on November 2, Rommel was down to thirty-five German and one hundred Italian tanks. The DAK had lost two-thirds of its troops.

Taking advantage of a temporary lull in the fighting on November 3, Rommel began a cautious withdrawal to Fuka, twenty miles to the west. The Italian troops in the south received priority in the retreat while the DAK and the Italian divisions in the north were to hold and then retire by stages. Fortunately, an Italian tanker docked at Benghazi, and the Luftwaffe arrived with 1,200 tons of gasoline for Rommel's getaway.

Then came another surprise. Just as his men prepared to leave the death trap, Rommel received a personal directive from Hitler. "Stand fast," the führer decreed. "Yield not a yard of ground, and throw every gun and every man into battle. . . . You can show them no other road than that to victory or death." Rommel regarded Hitler's order as complete madness, but he obeyed. Even the Desert Fox could not reverse the erosion of his army, however. The Italian divisions were collapsing, and the Panzers were beyond the peak of their endurance. Rommel had already lost 32,000 men, 450 tanks, all his 88s, three-fourths of his armored cars, and most of his artillery. He had to save the rest of his men from death or capture. Rommel wired Hitler that his command could hold no longer and that it was retreating. A day later, Hitler authorized the withdrawal, which was already well under way. Just as Montgomery had predicted, victory came to the Eighth Army on November 4.

Now the Axis forces hurried westward along the coastal road and the desert. Tanks and cars scurried to outpace the pursuing armor of the enemy and to avoid the RAF strafing. Men on foot raced to catch up with already crammed vehicles. About thirty thousand ground troops fell behind and were captured. Ramcke's paratroop brigade was completely cut off. It tramped four days over the wasteland until by luck the brigade captured an enemy truck convoy and joined Rommel at Fuka. The 222nd Paratroop Brigade fought its way out of traps, captured British trucks, and drove two hundred miles to reach safety.

In a scene that could have been written for a Hollywood movie, Thoma found himself far behind with fifteen tanks.

Putting on his badges and decorations, Thoma led his Panzers in one last crazy charge against incredible odds. When his own tank was demolished, Thoma leaped out of the burning hulk. He tied his checkered scarf carefully, brushed the dirt off his uniform, clutched his dispatch case, and waited to be captured. After interrogation by British intelligence, Thoma was invited by Montgomery to dine in his tent, where the two enemy generals spent the evening quietly discussing the battle.

Rommel's retreat to Fuka began in panic, but later the withdrawal was orderly. The Afrika Korps had the advantage of traveling along the coastal road, just ahead of a torrential rain that slowed their pursuers. Though the DAK was limping in defeat, it still had sharp teeth. As one unit fought, the others retreated. Then another regiment halted to permit the rear guard to catch up. Rommel's engineers were ingenious in delaying the Eighth by mining roads, blowing up embankments, digging antitank ditches, and setting thousands of booby traps in wells, doors, houses, and burned trucks.

Leaving Fuka on November 6, Rommel's men reached Mersa Matruh on November 7, Gazala on November 12, and Mersa Brega on November 15. It was a remarkable retreat, and it was conducted with skill. As a result of Rommel's cunning, his thirty-two tanks managed to prevent four flanking attempts by enemy armored brigades from the desert. Rommel eluded Montgomery along the entire Libyan coast. After fleeing 1,400 miles from El Alamein, the DAK reached the sanctuary of Tunisia on February 2, 1943, with the Eighth Army far behind. Rommel had lost half his army and all his guns; only twenty tanks were still functioning.

The Eighth failed to catch Rommel for several reasons: it was exhausted after the Battle of El Alamein; it was short of fuel; staff work during the pursuit was poor; and Montgomery was too cautious. Yet, unquestionably, Montgomery had won a splendid victory at El Alamein. To celebrate the long-awaited triumph, Churchill ordered that church bells in the British Isles, silent for years, peal out the news to the world.

After years of defeat in the desert, the British and their Commonwealth Allies had finally driven the Afrika Korps from Egypt, thanks to material superiority and Montgomery's leadership. The tide was turning against the Axis. Now, slowly and methodically, Montgomery led the Eighth to attack Rommel's new stronghold in Tunisia—the Mareth Line.

13
THE LAST CAMPAIGN

IN EARLY February 1943 the Afrika Korps found sanctuary at the Mareth Line, 110 miles inside southern Tunisia. Flanked by the sea and the Matmata Hills, these French-built defenses presented a difficult barrier to the slow-moving Eighth Army. The long withdrawal from El Alamein was over. The desert war had ended. Now the fight for mountainous Tunisia was the final phase of the struggle for North Africa.

Rommel was demoralized over the retreat. His health was poor. He lacked logistical support, and he quarreled with Rome and Berlin about strategy. Tunisia seemed like a lost cause, but Hitler refused to evacuate the Axis armies. After resting briefly in Germany and receiving assurance of weapons and reinforcements, Rommel tried to recover the initiative and to hold Tunisia.

As the DAK had retired across Libya, the Axis dictators had poured troops and equipment into Tunis and Bizerte. These soldiers protected Rommel's command from the west, but Hitler and Mussolini had another plan for them as well: to eject the Torch armies from Tunisia. They wanted to prevent General Dwight Eisenhower's Allied troops from seizing Tunisia's ports, and using them as a springboard for an invasion of Italy.

On November 15, 1942, the Allies began their five-hundred-mile overland drive to the Tunisian coast before the Axis could establish a bridgehead. Britain's First Army penetrated from the north; the United States Second Corps approached from the west. Weather, terrain, and supply problems prevented both forces from reaching their objectives. The British were repulsed by the enemy on December 2, and the Americans met defeat on December 25.

Inasmuch as the Eighth Army was still a hundred miles from the Mareth Line, Rommel had two weeks to smash the inexperienced American army before dealing with Montgomery. Leaving his Italian infantry and the Fifteenth Panzer Division at Mareth under General Giovanni Messe, Rommel led the rest of the DAK through Maknassy Pass. He and Colonel General Hans-Jürgen von Arnim planned to surprise the American Second Corps as it lay scattered over the plains east of the Western Dorsal. On February 13 Arnim's Panzers pushed through Faid Pass and captured Sidi Bou Zid and Sbeitla from the Americans. Rommel also moved quickly. By February 15 he held Guettar, Gafsa, and Feriana. The Axis armies were ready to hurl the Allies from the Western Dorsal and back into Algeria.

Unfortunately for Rommel, he was not supreme commander in Tunisia. He shared the authority with another German general, Arnim—his enemy for twenty years—and the two did not agree on strategy. As a result, each Axis army acted independently. Arnim wanted to consolidate his grip on the Western Dorsal before advancing. Rommel was more daring. He planned to drive through Kasserine Pass, smash the American Second Corps, grab the American bases, and push into northeast Algeria. As a compromise, Arnim promised to send Rommel part of his Tenth Panzer Division.

At Kasserine Pass, Rommel demonstrated his tactical skills. After his assault group stalled because of the rocky terrain and stiff American resistance, Rommel led tanks and motorized infantry through Kasserine in a brilliant attack that shattered the American defenses. Wet and weary, his men seem inspired, as in the old days in Libya.

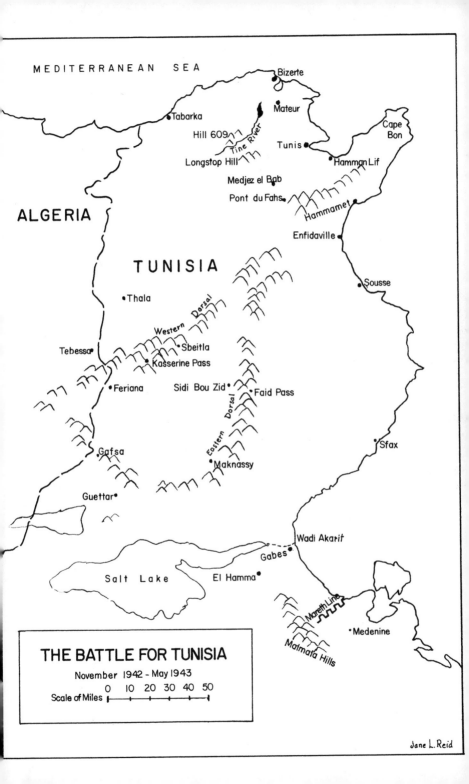

MEDITERRANEAN SEA

Bizerte

Mateur

Tabarka

Hill 609

Longstop Hill

Tine River

Tunis

Cape Bon

Hamman Lif

Medjez el Bab

Pont du Fahs

Hammamet

ALGERIA

Enfidaville

TUNISIA

Sousse

Thala

Western Dorsal

Tebessa

Sbeitla

Kasserine Pass

Feriana

Sidi Bou Zid

Faid Pass

Eastern Dorsal

Gafsa

Maknassy

Sfax

Guettar

Wadi Akarit

Gabes

Salt Lake

El Hamma

Mareth Line

Medenine

Matmata Hills

THE BATTLE FOR TUNISIA

November 1942 - May 1943

0   10 20 30 40 50

Scale of Miles

Jane L. Reid

Now close to a decisive victory as the Second Corps retreated in panic to Tebessa and Thala, Rommel hurried his force northward. A decisive victory was within his grasp, but a number of factors caused him to halt: the Twenty-first Panzer Division lost Sbeitla because of torrents of rain and seas of mud, and thus Rommel's flank was exposed; the Italian Centauro Armored Division lagged behind at Feriana; the Americans and British threw in more guns and tanks to hold the road to Thala. Furthermore, Rommel realized that the Americans had excellent artillery and that in mountain fighting they were superior to his own troops. When Arnim failed to send the promised one hundred tanks, Rommel terminated his offensive. Like a tired marathon runner approaching the final tape, Rommel nearly collapsed from physical strain, the uncertainties of a split command structure, and the lack of support in Berlin. Yet at Kasserine Pass, he had dealt the Second Corps a stunning blow: he captured four thousand Americans, knocked out two hundred tanks, and destroyed sixty guns. This was the first contest between American GIs and Rommel's professionals. Eisenhower's staff was stunned by the near-disaster, but the Torch armies were learning to fight.

Rommel realized that his time in Africa was nearly over. He suffered from rheumatism, nervous exhaustion, and heart trouble. The 346,000 Axis troops in Tunisia needed vast quantities of supplies. But half of the Italian ships bound for Tunisia were sunk in January and February, and the Luftwaffe flew in only small quantities of fuel. The embittered field marshal realized that he had lost Hitler's confidence and that the high command wanted him on sick leave. But the Desert Fox had an old score to settle. Before he left Africa, he wanted to humiliate Montgomery, the only general who had beaten him.

In late February, the Eighth Army stood at Medenine, twenty-five miles south of the Mareth Line. The terrain prevented Rommel from trying a surprise. He proposed an attack at the north and south of the enemy positions. Berlin disagreed with his strategy, however, and Messe's simpler plan was adopted. Disgusted with the quarreling, Rommel permitted Messe to arrange the battle. While the assault was under way, Rommel watched from a hill fifteen miles away.

On March 7, four Italian infantry divisions and 150 tanks crossed the broad flat plain to Medenine. This time the Axis force charged without proper reconnaissance and encountered murderous fire from the Eighth's 400 tanks and 500 guns. So devastating was the shelling that one-third of Rommel's armor was demolished within hours. Montgomery's seasoned veterans could hardly believe that the DAK and the Italian units made such blunders. Obviously, the Fox's old magic was missing in this fight. Like a tired old boxer going through the motions, Rommel was worn out and called off the operation by evening. His last campaign for Africa was a complete failure. On the verge of collapse, on March 9 Rommel left Tunisia, never to return. Unable to convince Hitler to evacuate Tunisia, or to withdraw Messe's and Arnim's armies to Enfidaville on the coast, Rommel took a long sick leave.

Even without its leader, the Afrika Korps fought well in a increasingly desperate situation. Field Marshal Harold Alexander, Eisenhower's commander, had nineteen well-equipped divisions and 1,000 tanks against fifteen worn-out divisions of the Axis with 150 tanks. The future was grim for the German and Italian soldiers as the Allied armies recovered the Western Dorsal, pressed closer to the Eastern Dorsal, and moved up from the south.

Montgomery made the next decisive move. On March 20 he tried to crack the Mareth Line with a frontal assault. After three days of heavy losses, he shifted pressure with a tank force that he had sent through the hills. British armor tore through the Tebega Gap, swept through to El Hamma, and smashed the Mareth Line at its weak southern tip.

Messe retreated to the next defensive line—the Wadi Akarit. Although his troops made a defiant stand here, the

Italian general had insufficient mines, guns, wire, and tank traps to repel the Eighth Army. On April 6 Montgomery's divisions cracked the Akarit Line. The next day, Messe led his command north to Enfidaville, just as Rommel had urged weeks before. Meanwhile, the Torch armies penetrated to the Eastern Dorsal. By March 25 the Americans had taken Gafsa and Guettar and joined the Eighth in the south. In the north, the British First Army finally captured a major obstacle, Longstop Hill, on April 24. As May began, the American Second Corps, now combat-wise, fought four bloody days to seize Hill 609 from the Germans.

The Axis forces were surrounded in their last-ditch effort to hold a bridgehead at Tunis, Cape Bon, and Enfidaville. Hit from the north, the west, and the south, Arnim and Messe were forced back to the sea. The last major fight for the DAK occurred on April 28. Tunis fell on May 7 to the British Seventh Armored Division—the Desert Rats of the early campaigns. Bizerte toppled on May 8, and Messe and Arnim surrendered their 300,000 troops on May 12.

On May 13 General Hans Cramer, the last commander of the Afrika Korps, sent a final message to Rommel in Berlin: "Ammunition shot off. Arms and equipment destroyed. In accordance with orders received, Afrika Korps fought itself to the condition where it can fight no more. The German Afrika Korps must rise again. Heia safari!" On May 19, 1943, as the last Axis troops were rounded up on Cape Bon, Alexander cabled Churchill: "All enemy resistance has ceased. We are masters of North Africa." The campaign that had begun in July 1940 on the Egyptian border was finally over.

And what happened to Rommel? Because of supposed failures in Tunisia, the state of his health, and disagreements with superiors, he was a field marshal in temporary cold storage. He recuperated quickly, however, and his services were needed in a new theater of war. The Allies invaded Sicily on July 8. Mussolini was overthrown and then killed on July 27. The Americans landed in Naples on September 8 and, soon after that, Italy quit the war. Rommel's assignment during the summer and early autumn of 1943 was to guard northern Italy while Kesselring defended southern Italy. But in another debate about strategy to halt the Allied advance to Rome, Rommel lost the argument. On October 21 he was sent to France.

The Germans were toiling to build an Atlantic Wall in order to repel a huge Allied amphibious operation from Britain expected in mid-1944. Rommel's task was to create an impenetrable Death Zone, six miles deep, from Denmark through northern France. He devised ingenious methods of preventing the enemy from establishing beachheads on the coast. The mistakes made by German intelligence in determining the place of the D day invasion on June 6, 1944, the errors made by Hitler and his generals in deploying troops, and the successful penetration by Eisenhower's divisions into France and Belgium by July are another phase of the war.

As the Germans were losing in Russia, Italy, and France during the summer of 1944, it is fascinating to follow Rommel's career. Like many of his military and civilian associates, he was certain by late June that Germany had lost the war. He wondered how he could convince Hitler to negotiate an armistice. Rommel hesitated to mention the subject to the crazed dictator, for such a suggestion could lead to his own execution and that of his family. Like many Wehrmacht generals, Rommel saw no alternative but to fight to the bitter end. Rommel's name, however, was used, without his knowledge, by men who were plotting to kill Hitler.

In July 1944 the plotters—a small group of prominent German generals and politicians—were planning to assassinate Hitler so as to allow Germany to avoid total destruction. Many conspirators were Rommel's friends and acquaintances. To convince potential supporters that Rommel backed the scheme, the plotters frequently mentioned that he was a member of the inner circle. But Rommel was not involved in the effort. He knew nothing of the effort to kill Hitler, and he maintained his loyalty to the führer.

While the arrangements to eliminate Hitler were being

completed, Rommel was seriously injured. Two low-flying Spitfires spotted his car and opened fire as he drove from a conference in Normandy on July 17. The car was demolished, and Rommel, with multiple skull fractures, spent a month in the hospital. In mid-August, he returned home to Swabia to recuperate.

In the meantime, the plot to kill Hitler—by detonating a bomb at his headquarters in East Prussia—had failed. Hitler survived the explosion and swore vengeance on his would-be murderers.

In a horrible purge, Hitler's gestapo and secret police imprisoned thousands of suspects and executed hundreds of innocent victims. Virtually all the plotters were captured, questioned, and tortured. By August 12 Hitler was convinced that Rommel had supported the assassination attempt. After pondering the matter for weeks, Hitler finally decided that Rommel had to die as a traitor to the Third Reich.

On October 13, while still expecting to receive command of an army on the Russian front, Rommel was confronted at his home by Hitler's gestapo. For the first time, the Desert Fox learned that he was suspected of treason and that he was to die as a traitor. He was offered the choice of being executed or committing suicide. After a hasty farewell to his wife and son, Rommel drove off in a car with his visitors. A few minutes later, he was given poison. He swallowed the cyanide and died within seconds. Rommel had chosen the hero's gateway to Valhalla, the mythical heaven for warriors. How ironic that Rommel who had survived bombs, shells, bullets, mines, and grenades in dozens of campaigns should die because of a fumbled conspiracy in which he had no part. On October 18, 1944, Rommel was given a state funeral in Berlin worthy of a famed field marshal of the Third Reich. By May 1945 Germany was in ruins; Hitler had committed suicide; the war in Europe was over.

As a result of his exploits and those of his men, Rommel remains a legend. He is the most admired German general of

World War II. In memory of the Desert Fox a simple wooden cross marks his grave in Herrlingen, Germany. Near Tobruk on the Via Balbia stands a stone monument commemorating the dead of the DAK, and this marker is also a tribute to Rommel. Once a year, veterans of the Afrika Korps visit this site. These proud men—now gray and wrinkled with age—can remember their distinguished commander ordering them to mount up for another adventure in the desert.

BIBLIOGRAPHY

Barnett, Correlli. *The Desert Generals.* New York: Viking, 1961.

Bergot, Erwan. *The Afrika Korps.* Translated by Richard Barry. London: Wingate, 1972.

Collier, Richard. *The War in the Desert.* New York: Time-Life Books, 1977.

Connell, John. *Auchinleck.* London: Cassell, 1959.

Forty, George. *The Desert Rats at War.* London: Allen, 1975.

Irving, David. *The Trail of the Fox.* New York: Dutton, 1977.

Jackson, W.G.F. *The Battle for North Africa 1940–1943.* New York: Mason/Charter, 1975.

Jones, Vincent. *Operation Torch.* New York: Ballantine Books, 1972.

Lewin, Ronald. *Rommel as Military Commander.* New York: Van Nostrand Reinhold, 1968.

———. *Montgomery as Military Commander.* New York: Stein & Day, 1971.

———. *Ultra Goes to War.* New York: McGraw Hill, 1978.

Lucas, James. *The Panzer Army in Africa.* San Rafael, Calif.: Presidio Press, 1977.

Majdalany, Fred. *The Battle of El Alamein.* New York: Lippincott, 1965.

Mellenthin, Friedrich von. *Panzer Battles.* Translated by H. Betzler. Norman: University of Oklahoma Press, 1975.

Moorehead, Alan. *The March of Tunis: The North African War 1940–1943.* New York: Harper, 1943.

185

Schmidt, Heinz Werner. *With Rommel in the Desert.* London: Harrap, 1951.

Swinson, Arthur. *The Raiders: Desert Strike Force.* New York: Ballantine Books, 1968.

Young, Desmond. *Rommel: The Desert Fox.* New York: Harper, 1950.

INDEX

Afrika Korps, 19; birth of, 26, 35, 37; comradeship with British, 111–114; environmental adaptation of, 50, 108–117; in Egypt, 57, 78–79, 100–102, 133–174; in fight for Tobruk, 53–67, 69, 72, 77–107, 123, 129–132; first campaign of, 38–52; and Italy, *see* Italy; last campaign of, 175–180; in Libya, 24–26, 37–52, 53–67, 69, 72, 77–107, 123, 129–132; logistics of, *see* Logistics; in Operation Battleaxe, 68–73; in Operation Crusader, 81–107; reputation of, 50, 52, 74; Rommel assigned to, 35, 37. *See also* Rommel

Alam el Halfa, 150–157

Algeria, 35, 156

Allies. *See names of countries*

Austria, German occupation of, 31

Axis. *See names of countries*

Bardia, 24

Battle techniques: of Montgomery, 145–146, 148, 149–152, 163–164; of Rommel, 34, 39, 44, 64, 67, 75–77, 79–80, 121, 134, 145, 157

Belgium, 32, 33

Benghazi, 46, 49, 54

Bir Hacheim, 128, 129

Blitzkrieg, 31–32

Bloody Sunday, 98, 100

Blue Max, 29

Britain: comradeship with Afrika Korps, 111–114; in East Africa, 19–22, 26, 57, 58; in Egypt, 57, 78–79, 100–102, 133–174; environmental adaptation of, 108–117; in fight for Tobruk, 53–67, 69, 72, 77–107, 123, 129–132; in first Afrika Korps campaign, 38–52; in Libya, 24–26, 37–52, 53–67, 69, 72, 77–107, 123, 129–132; logistics of, *see* Logis-

ABOUT THE AUTHOR

RICHARD BLANCO served as an airplane mechanic in the Army Air Force before graduating from the University of Maryland. He has a Ph.D. in history from Case-Western Reserve University. He has taught in high school and several colleges and presently teaches at the State University of New York in Brockport, New York. Mr. Blanco has written a number of articles on medical and military history and two biographies of physicians.